CONOR McCORMICK AND
BRICE DICKSON

WITH A FOREWORD
BY DAME SIOBHAN KEEGAN

THE COURT OF APPEAL
IN NORTHERN IRELAND

B BRISTOL
UNIVERSITY
PRESS

First published in Great Britain in 2025 by

Bristol University Press
University of Bristol
1–9 Old Park Hill
Bristol
BS2 8BB
UK
t: +44 (0)117 374 6645
e: bup-info@bristol.ac.uk

Details of international sales and distribution partners are available at
bristoluniversitypress.co.uk

British Library Cataloguing in Publication Data
A catalogue record for this book is available from the British Library

ISBN 978-1-5292-4701-5 paperback
ISBN 978-1-5292-4174-7 ePub
ISBN 978-1-5292-4175-4 OA PDF

Cover design: Blu inc
Front cover image: Richard Summerville

Contents

List of Tables

Acknowledgements

We have incurred deep debts of gratitude to five groups of people in the course of writing this book.

First, we owe the Lady Chief Justice and President of the Court of Appeal in Northern Ireland, Dame Siobhan Keegan, extensive thanks for trusting, supporting, and facilitating us with our endeavours, and for writing such a generous Foreword to this text. Likewise, we are indebted to several members of staff from within the Lady Chief Justice's Office and the Office of the Court of Appeal. We are particularly grateful to Alison Houston and Amanda Climie for their unstinting assistance. In addition, we owe weighty thanks to the judges who were willing to speak to us about this project. Though we cannot name them, on account of interviewee anonymity, we wish to express our emphatic gratitude to each and every judge concerned.

Second, we owe thanks to Mark Coen and Noel McGrath, from the UCD Sutherland School of Law, for an opportunity to present some of the work underpinning this volume at a conference titled 'A New Intermediate Appellate Court: Ten Years of the Court of Appeal of Ireland' in University College Dublin on 3–4 May 2023. Their invitation to contribute to that conference was the trigger which set in train the research project which has led to this book. We are also grateful to the participants at that conference for the feedback and motivation they shared.

Third, we owe thanks to a broad range of lawyers and academics who have assisted us – directly and indirectly – with various aspects of the project. We record our thanks, in particular, to Gordon Anthony, Kevin Brown, Anna Bryson, David Capper, Anurag Deb, Arthur Harvey, David Lavery, Christopher McCrudden, Oswyn Paulin, John Stannard, Graham Truesdale, and John Wilson. This is a non-exhaustive list!

Fourth, we owe thanks to everyone at Bristol University Press for their assistance in the editing and production of this publication. Helen Davis, Grace Carroll, Bahar Celik Muller, and Phylicia Ulibarri-Eglite have all been notably helpful at various stages of the process, together with Dawn Preston of Newgen Publishing UK. We also owe thanks to the anonymous academic peers who conscientiously reviewed our book proposal for the Press, as well as the anonymous reviewer who reviewed our first full draft. Moreover, we wish to thank Richard Summerville, from the School of Law at Queen's University Belfast, for capturing the Court of Appeal so well in the photograph which graces the cover of the book.

Fifth, we owe thanks to our family and friends for their encouragement and indulgences. Above all, James Nelson and Patricia Mallon.

Although the text which follows should not be read as having been endorsed by any of our many creditors – as it represents our independent assessments alone – we are certain that it has been enriched by their investments.

Foreword

Dame Siobhan Keegan
Lady Chief Justice of Northern Ireland and
President of the Court of Appeal in Northern Ireland

The Court of Appeal in Northern Ireland, when first established in 1921, consisted of Sir Denis Henry, the first Lord Chief Justice of Northern Ireland, and two Lords Justices of Appeal. It dealt with a total of 14 cases in its first year. The Court has evolved significantly since then both in terms of the number of Lords Justices and High Court judges who sit and hear appeals but also in the caseloads dealt with each year. This book provides a comprehensive account and description of the Court, and particularly its work over the past 25 years. It will be beneficial for lawyers, students, academics, and readers who are appearing before the Court or who are interested in how the important work of the Court has contributed to the legal and political landscape within this jurisdiction.

It is fascinating to see how historical records can illuminate how the judges of the Court of Appeal were appointed and, in particular, how the religious and political composition was something which was engineered and indeed comprehensively documented. This book is fascinating from a historical perspective and readers will benefit from tracing how the Court operated in the early stages, as compared with the present day.

The authors give the reader an insight into the work of the Court of Appeal, the challenges, the nature of the work, and the difficulties associated with the work of an appellate court in a small jurisdiction. I welcome this esteemed work by Dr Conor McCormick and Professor Brice Dickson. They have provided a meticulous portrait of the Court of Appeal in Northern Ireland which I am pleased they recognise as 'a highly professionalised and self-aware judicial body … [and] a singular institution operating "a distinct jurisdiction" for "a different place"'.

ONE

Introduction

The public doorways to the Court of Appeal in Northern Ireland are physically located on the left-hand side of the Great Hall in the Royal Courts of Justice, Belfast, which can be accessed by way of a security checkpoint at the gated Chichester Street entrance. The public gallery is usually occupied by litigants involved in the cases listed to be heard – occasionally with a few members of the public – who sit behind a wooden barrier demarcating an area of the room which is for the exclusive use of practising lawyers. Junior counsel will usually sit in the row closest to the public, senior counsel in the row ahead. All will face the judges' bench, with the back of their bewigged heads to the gallery. In front of the barristers, solicitors and paralegals will normally be seated on benches facing in the direction of the public gallery, taking notes and passing papers to counsel. Behind them, court clerks will be stationed at a table with computers through which they maintain the Court's records. Behind the clerks, two or three judges' chairs will be teed up across the bench. Tipstaves, who announce that a hearing is about to begin and assist the court with errands of all sorts, are likely to be positioned at the ends of the bench. In a box on one side of the courtroom, journalists may be readying themselves to write a report of the proceedings. Alternatively, they may be observing the Court from another location altogether by way of a digitally streamed 'Sightlink' channel. If so, their names will be displayed on some of the screens that are installed on desks throughout the room. In a box on the other side of the room, there may be a judicial assistant preparing to watch the proceedings before discussing them with the Court afterwards. Regularly rotating security guards will be surveying everyone alertly from different corners. When the Court is called into session, two or three of its judges will normally enter the room through doorways at the back. The presiding judge for each case will sit in the centre of the bench and orchestrate the proceedings from then on. The next most senior judge will sit to the presiding judge's right and the third judge, if there is one, to the left.

The principal aims of this book are to explain how the Court of Appeal has evolved into the important organ of justice that it is today, to demystify what it does when it is invited to reconsider decisions taken by courts and tribunals further down the judicial hierarchy in Northern Ireland, and to establish whether it could perform its role as an intermediate appellate court more effectively in any way. As such, the following text is intended to make it easier to appear before or follow the Court of Appeal – regardless of whether you are a solicitor, barrister, judicial assistant, law student, or interested onlooker – and to inform the judges themselves of how the Court of Appeal is perceived from a scholarly point of view.

To achieve these aims, we have carried out an extensive programme of research underpinned by five main methods of investigation and analysis. First, we have studied a range of archival documents relating to the historical development of the Court by way of several visits to the Public Records Office of Northern Ireland in Belfast and the National Archives at Kew Gardens in London. Second, we have compiled and examined a complete database of the publicly reported judgments handed down by the Court of Appeal over the past 25 years. Our doctrinal analysis of conspicuous cases has been enriched by reading targeted batches of secondary sources such as journal articles and newspaper reports. Third, we have collated a number of statistics relating to the operation of the Court. Some of these were obtained from publicly available online repositories, while others were helpfully supplied by the Lady Chief Justice's Office. Fourth, and again with the support of the Lady Chief Justice's Office, we have observed the Court of Appeal in action by attending an assortment of proceedings before it, both civil and criminal. Fifth, and complementing the ethnographic information we obtained from our observations of the Court in action, we have interviewed a broadly representative sample of the judges who have sat in the Court of Appeal in recent years. In line with the principles of academic ethics underpinning our interviews, the precise identity of each interviewee is not disclosed in the course of the book, but we can share that the pool of seven judges we spoke to were drawn from both the High Court and the permanent membership of the Court of Appeal. Some were still in office; some were retired. We have anonymised those we quote as 'J1', 'J2', 'J3', and so on. In addition to these formal interviews, we have had the good fortune of having informal discussions about the Court with a variety of legal professionals. These included solicitors and barristers with experience of appearing before the Court, current and former officials, and other interested academics.

Our multi-layered approach to the methodology underpinning this book is one of the features which sets it apart from other books in the same genre. Thus, while we have benefitted enormously from consulting the academic literature on other appellate courts in the UK, on the legal history of Northern Ireland, on the reasoning of particular judgments, on the Court's contribution to particular fields of law, and on the practice and procedure of the Court from a practitioner's point of view, we believe that the present volume constitutes a significant contribution to existing knowledge about the Court. The nature of that contribution will be revealed incrementally by way of seven substantive chapters and a short conclusion.

In Chapter 2, we provide an outline of how the Court of Appeal was first established and chart several significant turning points in its subsequent development. Those turning points include the creation and subsequent abolition of a separate Court of Criminal Appeal in 1930 and 1978, a fundamental restructuring of the Court's governing framework in 1978, and a suite of gradual modifications to the process for appointing Court of Appeal judges. In Chapter 3, we offer a bird's-eye view of the business that has been conducted by the Court of Appeal over the past 25 years, as a precursor to the qualitative analysis of that business in subsequent chapters. The chapter begins by providing a statistical breakdown of the cases which have been 'disposed of' between 1999 and 2023 and the rather smaller number of cases which have been 'reported' in some way. It then examines the contributions of individual judges to the Court of Appeal on a statistical basis and sets out some interesting trends such as the increasing frequency with which retired and puisne judges have been sitting, and the increasing use of two-person appeal panels.

Chapter 4 furnishes a detailed evaluation of the Court's civil business. It opens with a statistical overview of civil appeal types in Northern Ireland before proffering a qualitative analysis of key cases which are discussed in line with the different sources of civil appeals, beginning with appeals from the High Court (including a separate section on appeals in judicial review cases) and ending with appeals by way of case stated or on a point of law. Chapter 5 contains similar analyses but with a focus on the criminal business of the Court. Like the previous chapter, it presents an analysis of key cases in categories reflecting the various sources of appeals, encompassing appeals against conviction and/or sentence from the Crown Court (where many of the cases involving serious criminal offences are tried by county court, not High Court, judges), appeals by way of case stated from an inferior court (that is, a magistrates' court or a county court), references by the Director of Public

Prosecutions claiming that a sentence imposed by a lower court was unduly lenient, and references by the Criminal Cases Review Commission in cases where there has possibly been a miscarriage of justice.

In Chapter 6, we delineate our appraisal of the most conspicuous cases that have been heard by the Court of Appeal over the past quarter of a century. We highlight various decisions that have formed part of the legal Zeitgeist in Northern Ireland because of their precedential influence together with other decisions which have attracted a significant degree of attention from the wider public. The chapter covers politically sensitive cases that have arisen in respect of the Belfast (Good Friday) Agreement of 1998 and its legislative offspring, as well as equally sensitive cases that have come about as a consequence of Brexit. It further examines the most notable human rights law cases that have been decided by the Court in the context of litigation arising out of Northern Ireland's 'troubles', alongside other human rights law cases that have attracted societal interest in recent times.

Chapter 7 examines how the UK Supreme Court and its predecessor (the Appellate Committee of the House of Lords) have responded to appeals from the Court of Appeal in Northern Ireland. It incorporates analyses of 'leave/permission to appeal' decisions and of substantive judgments in cases for which leave/permission was granted either by the Court of Appeal itself (a rare occurrence) or by a three-person panel of the Lords or the Supreme Court (which is the norm). We comment on the success rate of these appeals and on their subject matter. Finally, in Chapter 8 we unveil various findings from our judicial interviews. We examine the judges' views on three groups of issues in turn, highlighting policy areas where there seems to be a consensus in favour of either conservation or reform, in addition to areas where the judges' views vary. The three issues we explore are the legislative framework within which the Court of Appeal operates, the

Court's practices and procedures, and the role of the Court's President (the Chief Justice).

Emerging from this multidimensional study is, we hope, a portrait of the Court of Appeal in Northern Ireland which is both revelatory and reassuring. We sketch a thumbnail version of that portrait in the concluding chapter.

TWO

The Origins of the Court

2.1 Introduction

This chapter charts the genesis of the Court of Appeal in Northern Ireland before outlining how the Court has evolved in several fundamental respects over time. In the first section of the chapter, we assess the starting position of the Court by examining the Supreme Court of Judicature Act (Ireland) 1877 and the Government of Ireland Act 1920. We explain, in particular, how the 1920 Act originally established three courts: the Supreme Court of Judicature of Southern Ireland, the Supreme Court of Judicature of Northern Ireland, and a court having appellate jurisdiction throughout the whole of Ireland called the High Court of Appeal. The remainder of the first sub-section focuses on the only surviving Court established under the 1920 Act, namely, the Court of Appeal in Northern Ireland. We explore how that Court was established in practical terms under the leadership of its first President, Sir Denis Henry, and the roles played by its first Lords Justices, Sir William Moore and Sir James Andrews.

In the second section of the chapter, we turn our attention to some of the most significant changes to the governance of the Court of Appeal since its establishment. We explain that two key turning points in the legislative framework governing the structure and jurisdiction of the Court occurred in 1930 and 1978. In 1930, an Act was passed by the UK Parliament which created a new Court of Criminal Appeal that was separate from the Supreme Court of Judicature of Northern Ireland but staffed by all the same judges. In 1978, the Court of Criminal Appeal was abolished in tandem with the introduction of several fundamental changes to the overall court structure in Northern Ireland. We analyse the rationale for each of these significant developments. Finally, in the third section of the chapter, we recount the changing nature of the system that has been employed to determine the membership of the Court. We chronicle archival evidence which shows that a politicised judicial appointments system gradually gave way to a significantly de-politicised system.

2.2 The starting position

Long before the partition of Ireland, the Supreme Court of Judicature Act (Ireland) 1877 had created a consolidated supreme court structure for the island which mimicked that which had been introduced to England and Wales by the Supreme Court of Judicature Acts of 1873 and 1875.[1] There was a High Court of Justice in Ireland with a King's Bench Division and a Chancery Division,[2] with appeals lying to a Court of Appeal in Ireland,[3] and from there to the Appellate Committee of the House of Lords at Westminster.[4] The High Court and the Court of Appeal together constituted the Supreme Court of Judicature in Ireland.[5] Interestingly, the immediately inoperative Government of Ireland Act 1914, which would have enabled home rule for Ireland as a whole,

---

[1] For a brief account of the judicial system that pertained in Ireland prior to the 1877 Act, see the *Report of the Committee on the Supreme Court of Judicature of Northern Ireland* (The MacDermott Report: Cmnd 4292, 1970), para 52.

[2] Supreme Court of Judicature Act (Ireland) 1877, s 6.

[3] Ibid, s 10.

[4] Appellate Jurisdiction Act 1876, s 3(3).

[5] Supreme Court of Judicature Act (Ireland) 1877, ss 4–5.

did not envisage any changes to the court structure introduced in 1877.[6]

In contrast, when the partition of Ireland was brought into effect at Westminster by the Government of Ireland Act 1920, and Northern Ireland itself was thus established as a legal entity separate from Southern Ireland for the first time,[7] a significantly different set of court arrangements was provided for. Under section 38 of the 1920 Act, the Supreme Court of Judicature in Ireland ceased to exist and was replaced by three new bodies, namely:

> a court having jurisdiction in Southern Ireland, to be called the Supreme Court of Judicature of Southern Ireland, a court having jurisdiction in Northern Ireland, to be called the Supreme Court of Judicature of Northern Ireland, and a court having appellate jurisdiction throughout the whole of Ireland, to be called the High Court of Appeal.

The Southern Ireland and Northern Ireland Supreme Courts of Judicature were similar in their structure, if not their overall size, given that the Southern Court was to have six puisne judges (or, until the existing Master of the Rolls retired, five puisne judges plus that office-holder), whereas the Northern Ireland Court would have only two puisne judges.[8] Structurally, however, each Supreme Court of Judicature consisted of a High Court and a Court of Appeal, with the Court of Appeal in each jurisdiction being presided over by a separate Lord Chief Justice and 'two ordinary judges' known as Lords Justices of Appeal.[9]

---

6   JAL McLean, 'Some Developments in Northern Ireland Since 1921' (1972) 23 *NILQ* 82, 82.

7   Government of Ireland Act 1920, s 1(2).

8   Ibid, s 39(2), Sch 7, Pt 1, para 1(1), and s 40(2), Sch 7, Pt 2, para 1(1).

9   Ibid, s 39(2), Sch 7, Pt 1, para 2(1), and s 40(2), Sch 7, Pt 2, para 2(1).

The Lords Chief Justices of Southern Ireland and Northern Ireland were members of the High Court of Appeal for Ireland *ex officio*, together with the Lord Chancellor of Ireland, who presided over the High Court of Appeal.[10] That bench could receive cases from both the Court of Appeal in Southern Ireland and the Court of Appeal in Northern Ireland,[11] and in this way it briefly 'interposed' between those Courts of Appeal and the Appellate Committee of the House of Lords[12] (which retained a closely prescribed jurisdiction to hear certain appeals from the High Court of Appeal).[13] However, the High Court of Appeal for Ireland was short-lived. Soon after the Southern Court of Appeal became inoperative following the formation of the Irish Free State in December 1922, the High Court of Appeal for Ireland was abolished and its jurisdiction as regards Northern Ireland was transferred to the Court of Appeal in Northern Ireland.[14] During its brief existence, the High Court of Appeal decided ten reported cases, including one in which the bench held that it was not bound by decisions of the former Court of Appeal which had been established under the 1877 Act.[15] Thus, while it lasted, the High Court of Appeal presided over by the Lord Chancellor of Ireland was plainly keen to emphasise that it was 'separate and distinct' from its predecessors, though it did resolve to 'consider with the utmost reverence and respect the decisions of [earlier] appellate courts'.[16]

---

[10] Ibid, s 42.

[11] Ibid, s 43.

[12] McLean, n 6, 86.

[13] Government of Ireland Act 1920, s 49.

[14] Irish Free State (Consequential Provisions) Act 1922, Sch 1, para 6.

[15] *Leyburn v Armagh County Council (No. 2)* [1922] 2 IR 58.

[16] Ibid. For historical details on how the Court of Appeal in Northern Ireland chose to treat precedents established by the courts which had previously exercised an equivalent jurisdiction in Ireland, and how it chose to treat precedents on analogous points of law decided by the Court of Appeal in England and Wales, see FH Newark, 'Law and Precedent

Before returning our focus to the Court of Appeal in Northern Ireland, it may be worth noting that, although it was short-lived, the business of the High Court of Appeal for Ireland certainly impacted on the workload of the newly created Lord Chief Justice and Lords Justices of Appeal in Northern Ireland when they were nominated to sit on it. A memorandum on the first year of the Supreme Court of Judicature of Northern Ireland reveals, for instance, that the Lord Chief Justice attended the High Court of Appeal in Dublin 'on four occasions during the year, and Lord Justice Andrews on six'.[17] In addition, it records that the High Court of Appeal 'sat once in Belfast on July 27th [1922], when the Lord Chancellor, the Lord Chief Justice of Ireland, and Lord Justice Moore sat to hear an appeal from the Chief Justice [of Northern Ireland] and Lord Justice Andrews'.[18] Had it existed for longer, it would have been interesting to observe the degree of judicial comity that might have evolved under this unusual appellate court structure.

Although it is tempting to review the formative years of the Supreme Court of Judicature of Northern Ireland as a whole, we must refrain from analysing the establishment of the High Court (which consisted originally of the Lord Chief Justice and two puisne judges)[19] and focus only on the Court of Appeal

---

in Northern Ireland' (1972) 23 *NILQ* 100. Also see *Parkinson v Watson* [1956] NI 1, a salient decision by the Court of Appeal which is not cited by Newark but which was brought to our attention by Anurag Deb. We refer to the Court's current approach to precedents in Chapter 3.

[17] *Memoranda on the setting up of the Supreme Court of Judicature in Northern Ireland, and other matters incidental thereto, 1st October, 1921–31st July, 1922,* 25, in the Public Records Office of Northern Ireland at T311/1.

[18] Ibid.

[19] Wilson and Brown JJ were the first puisne judges appointed to the High Court of Justice in Northern Ireland. The maximum number of puisne judges expanded to its current limit of 15 in several increments. The original maximum of 2 puisne judges was expanded to 4 by the Administration of Justice Act 1968, s 1(1)(d); it then increased to 5 under art 2 of the Maximum Number of Judges Order 1972, to 6 under the

(which, as mentioned earlier, consisted of the Lord Chief Justice and two Lords Justices of Appeal).[20] We will confine ourselves to the consideration of two interesting points about the practical formation of that Court. First, we will outline some details about the judges that were appointed to it. Second, we will offer a brief evaluation of the workload they faced.

2.2.1 The inaugural judges

The first Lord Chief Justice of Northern Ireland was Sir Denis Henry,[21] whose background as a Catholic unionist has been studied with renewed interest over recent years.[22]

Judicature (NI) Act 1978, s 2(1), to 7 under art 2 of the Maximum Number of Judges (NI) Order 1993, to 9 under art 2 of the Maximum Number of Judges (NI) Order 2001, to 10 under art 2 of the Maximum Number of Judges (NI) Order 2004; and finally to 15 under art 2 of the Maximum Number of Judges (NI) Order 2020. There are currently 11 puisne judges in post, the highest number to hold office at any one time to date.

[20] The maximum number of Lords/Ladies Justices of Appeal has been increased only once in the history of the Court of Appeal in Northern Ireland. It was expanded from 2 to 3 by art 3 of the Administration of Justice (NI) Order 1975, which amended the Government of Ireland Act 1920, Sch 7, Pt 2, para 2(1), but the current statutory basis for this limitation is s 3(1) of the Judicature (NI) Act 1978. We will later explore whether there is a now a good case for creating a fourth post. See Chapters 3 and 8.

[21] See Appendix A for a complete list of Sir Denis Henry's successors as Lord/Lady Chief Justice of Northern Ireland.

[22] Sir Declan Morgan, 'Centenary Lecture on the Lord Chief Justices of Northern Ireland' (8 December 2021), [10]-[26], available at www.judiciaryni.uk/publications/centenary-lecture-lord-chief-justices-northern-ireland-rt-hon-sir-declan-morgan-8; Éamon Phoenix, 'The Life and Career of Denis Henry (1864–1925): Barrister, Ulster Unionist Politician and First Lord Chief Justice of Northern Ireland' in Brice Dickson and Conor McCormick (eds), *The Judicial Mind: A Festschrift for Lord Kerr of Tonaghmore* (Hart Publishing 2021); AD McDonnell, *The Life of Sir Denis Henry: Catholic Unionist* (Ulster Historical Foundation 2000).

Indeed, Sir Denis's appointment as Lord Chief Justice has been described by one of his successors as 'the obvious choice' at least partly because the objective of Sir James Craig, who was one of the two people responsible for the appointment, 'was to ensure that the position ... was filled by someone who was committed to the unionist cause'.[23] Sir Denis had been a successful unionist MP (elected in 1916 and again in 1918) before becoming the Attorney General for Ireland between 1919 and 1921. Having chosen to assume the office of Lord Chief Justice 'in preference to a Lordship of Appeal which he was offered at just about the same time',[24] Sir Denis was sworn into office at Portrush Town Hall (seemingly because of 'the Lord Chancellor's holiday arrangements') on 15 August 1921,[25] which satisfied the statutory requirement that he should be in post not less than one month prior to 'the appointed day' on which the Supreme Court of Judicature would formally come into being, namely, 1 October 1921.[26] Through no shortage of effort on Sir Denis's part,[27] the Supreme Court of Judicature opened its doors shortly thereafter in the County Courthouse on the Crumlin Road of Belfast, where it continued to sit until the purpose-built Royal Courts of Justice that are still in use today were opened on Chichester Street in 1933.[28]

---

[23] Morgan, n 22, [22]. The other person responsible for his appointment was Ernest Clark, 'a civil servant with responsibility for the proposed wider Northern Ireland administration': ibid [21].

[24] Edward Jones, *Jones L.J.: His Life and Times − The Autobiography of The Right Honourable Sir Edward Jones* (The Impartial Reporter 1987) 91.

[25] Morgan, n 22, [23].

[26] Government of Ireland Act 1920, Sch 7, Pt 3, para 1(d); *Memoranda*, n 17, 1.

[27] *Memoranda*, n 17, 2–4.

[28] For a definitive account of how the Royal Courts of Justice were commissioned and constructed, see AR Hart, *A History of the Bar and Inn of Court of Northern Ireland* (The General Council of the Bar of Northern Ireland 2013) Ch 5.

The senior Lord Justice of Appeal to join Sir Denis Henry as a judge designated to form the first Court of Appeal in Northern Ireland was Sir William Moore,[29] who, prior to this appointment, was a puisne judge of the King's Bench Division of the High Court of Ireland and a former Unionist MP. Moore 'accepted appointment as the senior lord justice, being the only member of the southern judiciary who signified a desire to serve as a judge in Northern Ireland',[30] and indeed the only judge appointed to the new Supreme Court of Judicature for Northern Ireland who had any prior judicial experience.[31] It might be reasonably inferred from correspondence by the last Lord Chancellor of Ireland, Sir John Ross,[32] that Sir William was motivated to jump ships because he was not highly regarded by at least some of his judicial peers in Southern Ireland.[33] In addition, Sir Declan Morgan has observed that by the time Sir William was appointed (on 1 September 1921),[34] 'the risk to the establishment of Northern Ireland as an entity had disappeared and the worst of the sectarian violence had abated'.[35] That said, it has also been recorded by Sir Declan that the evidence in connection with Sir William's judicial contributions to the Court of Appeal in Northern Ireland shows he 'conducted the business of the court in an orderly

[29] See Appendix B for a complete list of Sir William Moore's successors as a Lord Justice of Appeal.

[30] Robert Carswell, 'Founding A Legal System: The Early Judiciary of Northern Ireland' in Felix M Larkin and Norma M Dawson (eds), *Lawyers, the Law and History* (Four Courts Press 2013) 20.

[31] Ibid 15.

[32] See Richard McBride, 'Sir John Ross Bt: The Last Lord Chancellor of Ireland 1921–1922' in David Capper, Conor McCormick, and Norma Dawson (eds), *Law and Constitutional Change* (Cambridge University Press, forthcoming).

[33] Morgan, n 22, [31].

[34] *Memoranda*, n 17, 1.

[35] Morgan, n 22, [34].

and professional manner'.[36] Sir Declan's lukewarm reading of the man confirms an earlier assessment by Lord Carswell,[37] though the latter account is perhaps a little more unflattering than the former.

The second Lord Justice appointed to complete the original Court of Appeal bench, long before a third Lord Justice was installed in 1975,[38] was Sir James Andrews.[39] Sir James, who hailed from a phenomenally successful family,[40] was appointed to this high office at the early age of 44 and stayed on the bench for approximately 30 years thereafter. For part of this time – namely, from 1937 onwards – Sir James was the Lord Chief Justice of Northern Ireland (having succeeded Sir William Moore, who had himself succeeded Sir Denis Henry from 1925 onwards). We note that following a review of Sir James's judgments from 1921 to 1925, Lord Carswell was unable to discern any pattern in his judicial opinions that might be said to 'demonstrate a particular judicial philosophy on his part', which is to say His Lordship detected neither any 'obvious liberalising or modernising' nor any 'undue inclination to conservative acceptance of established rules of law'.[41] Sir Edward Jones, on the other hand, was willing to qualify his otherwise gushing account of Sir James's judicial character by suggesting he may have been 'a little Crown minded', though Sir Edward was quick to add that if Sir James 'had any such

---

[36] Ibid.

[37] Carswell, n 30, 20–1.

[38] See n 20. The first Lord Justice of Appeal to be appointed to this third seat on the bench was Sir Ambrose McGonigal. See Appendix B for a complete list of his successors as a Lord Justice of Appeal.

[39] See Appendix B for a complete list of Sir James Andrews's successors as a Lord Justice of Appeal.

[40] His brother John was the second Prime Minister of Northern Ireland and his brother Thomas was Managing Director of the shipbuilding company responsible for designing RMS *Titanic*.

[41] Carswell, n 30, 22–3.

faults they were more than counterbalanced by his politeness, patience and thoroughness'.[42]

2.2.2 The initial workload

The volume of work carried out by the newly established Court of Appeal in Northern Ireland was remarkably slender, in that it heard just 14 cases between 1 October 1921 and 31 July 1922.[43] While a slow start could be expected as a result of the various practical challenges associated with its establishment, other evidence suggests that the Court was widely regarded as a broadly undemanding place to work. The sharpest qualitative account of its workload also comes from Lord Carswell, to whom we owe this free-spoken description:

> According to all accounts the plum jobs were in the court of appeal, which had by today's standards a very light list. It was customary in the early days for the two lords justices to sit on their own. It was not until the tenure of office of Sir James Andrews that the lord chief justice would preside regularly in the court of appeal. The junior lord justice was in charge of the civil bill appeals, which occupied him to some extent, but the reports indicate that the senior lord justice would generally prepare the leading judgment in appeals before the court of appeal, so the overall burden of work, if such it can be called, may have evened out.[44]

A similar impression emerges from this contemporary account of the Court's workload in 1925:

---

[42] Jones, n 24, 93.

[43] *Memoranda*, n 17, 32.

[44] Carswell, n 30, 17.

The Court of Appeal, it is true, does not get enough work to do, but as the expense of an Appeal to the House of Lords is, in most cases, prohibitive to an ordinary litigant, it is essential that the Court of Appeal should be maintained here as in 99% of the cases it is in fact the House of Lords for Northern Ireland.[45]

It is important to stress, however, that the inaugural judges were engaged to carry out judicial business beyond the jurisdiction of the Court of Appeal. For instance, as mentioned earlier, Henry LCJ and Moore and Andrews LJJ were required to sit on the High Court of Appeal for Ireland on several occasions during their first year in office, in addition to their extra-curial responsibilities relating to establishing the new court system. Moreover, archival records show that Moore and Andrews LJJ were relied upon by Henry LCJ 'to relieve the Puisne Judges' of historically under-reported business, including the cases arising from a newly established City Commission (which sat four times per year to obviate for Belfast prisoners 'the delay which used unavoidably to happen before trial at the next Assizes').[46] In addition, early law reports reveal that while Henry LCJ did not regularly preside over appeals, true to Lord Carswell's words, he did preside regularly over proceedings in the High Court.[47] As such, while subsequent appellate

---

[45] A letter from AN Anderson to the Prime Minister of Northern Ireland, 29 October 1925, in the Public Records Office of Northern Ireland at CAB/9/I/10/5. The opening paragraphs of the letter indicate that its message reflects a conversation between Anderson and the then Lord Chief Justice.

[46] *Memoranda*, n 17, 12.

[47] See, for example, *Adams v McGill* [1923] 2 IR 98, wherein Henry LCJ delivers a single judgment on behalf of the King's Bench Division of the High Court, or *Macaura v The Northern Assurance Company Ltd* [1925] NI 141, where Moore and Andrews LJJ dismiss an appeal against a judgment delivered by Henry LCJ on behalf of the King's Bench Division of the High Court.

court office-holders can still look upon the workload of the first Court of Appeal bench with justifiable envy,[48] we would emphasise that the negligibility of its caseload should not be taken to mean that its judges were exorbitantly indolent.

2.3 Significant changes to the governance of the Court

We will now examine some of the most significant developments that have taken place in connection with the governance of the Court of Appeal since its inauguration under the Government of Ireland Act 1920. There have been at least two key turning points in the legislative framework governing the structure and jurisdiction of the Court, which came about in 1930 and 1978. In the following two sub-sections, we shall consider each of those turning points together with some practical changes to the operation of the Court over the course of the years in question.

2.3.1 The (temporary) Court of Criminal Appeal

In 1930, Westminster passed the Criminal Appeal (NI) Act 1930, which had been introduced to Parliament by the UK Government following a request from the Northern Ireland Government that was accompanied with assurances that 'all parties in the Parliament of Northern Ireland desired the Bill which had been drafted in consultation with the legal authorities and with the Chief Justice'.[49] Notwithstanding this clear desire for change on the part of the devolved authorities, the Act had to be passed at Westminster because all matters

---

[48] See Chapter 3 for our analysis of the Court's caseload between 1999 and 2023.

[49] 'Ulster's Request: All Parties Desire the Bill' (*Belfast News Letter*, 4 July 1930), as excerpted and included in a Ministry of Home Affairs file about the Court of Criminal Appeal in Northern Ireland, in the Public Records Office of Northern Ireland at HA/8/278.

relating to the Supreme Court of Judicature of Northern Ireland were 'reserved' at the time.[50] Political demand for the Act was essentially predicated on the success of similar legislation passed for England and Wales in 1907,[51] and likewise for Scotland in 1926,[52] which created a new criminal appeals jurisdiction in each legal system. The 1930 Act did this for Northern Ireland by replicating the 1907 framework to a large extent; namely, by establishing a Court of Criminal Appeal which was separate from the Supreme Court of Judicature but staffed by all the same judges.[53]

Prior to the 1930 Act, anyone 'convicted on indictment in Northern Ireland who wished to appeal against conviction continued to invoke the powers of the Court of [sic] Crown Cases Reserved' as the 'jurisdiction of that Court had been preserved by the Judicature Act of 1877 and was ultimately vested in the Northern Ireland Court of Appeals [sic]'.[54] Northern Ireland's newly established Court of Criminal Appeal, on the other hand, could hear appeals from persons convicted on indictment against their conviction, sentence, or both.[55] Such appeals could be taken either on a point of law or, if leave was granted, on a question of fact or any other ground that appeared sufficient to the Court.[56] The 1930 Act in Northern Ireland differed from the 1907 Act in England and Wales in only one significant respect; namely, that it adopted some different language used in the 1926 Act for Scotland, which enabled the Northern Ireland Court of Criminal Appeal to quash or substitute sentences passed 'in any appeal, whether

---

[50] Government of Ireland Act 1920, s 47.
[51] Criminal Appeal Act 1907.
[52] Criminal Appeal (Scotland) Act 1926.
[53] Criminal Appeal (NI) Act 1930, s 1(1).
[54] McLean, n 6, 84. Some footnotes within these quotations have been removed.
[55] Criminal Appeal (NI) Act 1930, s 2.
[56] Ibid.

against conviction or sentence',[57] whereas in England and Wales if a person did not appeal against their sentence there was no power to alter it.

For our purposes, the most notable effect of the 1930 legislation was that it substantially expanded the powers and responsibilities of the Lord Chief Justice and the Lords Justices of Appeal in Northern Ireland, and indeed those of the puisne judges before long. This latter point is worth elaborating on here by reference to the fact that it became more and more commonplace for Lords Justices of Appeal and puisne judges of the High Court to be regarded as functionally 'interchangeable' in practice, such that by 1957 'they all took their turn on circuit and on criminal trials at Belfast city commission, the puisne judges regularly sat in the court of appeal and the lords justices would sit when required on civil trials and county court appeals'.[58]

An editorial essay published in an issue of the *Northern Ireland Legal Quarterly* for 1946 reveals, moreover, that even by then the 'small number of Judges in the Supreme Court of Northern Ireland' had made it 'inevitable that each Judge should be called upon to be an exponent of every branch of the law'.[59]

It should be emphasised that while the Court of Criminal Appeal dealt with appeals against convictions and sentences by persons convicted on indictment, the 'general' Court of Appeal in Northern Ireland retained jurisdiction over criminal appeals from county courts and magistrates' courts by way of case stated, as well as criminal appeals from lower courts (including the High Court) in proceedings for criminal contempt.[60] It was against this complicated backdrop that the Court of

---

[57] Ibid, s 3(3).

[58] Robert Carswell, '*Eheu Fugaces*: Fifty Years in the Northern Ireland Courts' in Daire Hogan and Colum Kenny (eds), *Changes in Practice and Law: A Selection of Essays by Members of the Legal Profession to Mark Twenty-Five Years of the Irish Legal History Society* (Four Courts Press 2013) 7.

[59] James R Lindsay, 'Editorial: A Review of the Supreme Court of Northern Ireland' (1946) 7 *NILQ* 3, 7.

[60] *Courts in Northern Ireland: The Future Pattern* (Cmnd, 6892), paras 22–3.

Criminal Appeal was abolished in 1978[61] in order to 'obviate the anomaly of having one type of criminal appeal heard by a court whose business is mainly civil and others by a court whose jurisdiction is exclusively criminal'.[62]

2.3.2 The (reconstituted) Supreme Court of Judicature

The Judicature (NI) Act 1978, which abolished the Court of Criminal Appeal, also fundamentally consolidated and restructured the jurisdiction of the 'general' Court of Appeal alongside many other reforms to the Northern Ireland court system. Papers prepared by the Northern Ireland Office at the time summarised the four major purposes of the Bill which became the 1978 Act in the following terms:

i)   The reconstitution of the Supreme Court of Judicature of Northern Ireland; the Court of Criminal Appeal, which is not part of the Supreme Court, will be abolished, and its jurisdiction absorbed by the Court of Appeal, which is and will continue to be part of the Supreme Court.

ii) [T]he establishment of a Crown Court, similar to that established in England and Wales under the Courts Act 1971, for the trial of all indictable offences throughout Northern Ireland. The existing courts of assize will be abolished, and the Crown Court will become part of the Supreme Court.

iii) [T]he establishment of a unified Court Service, comprising staff of the three court services which exist separately at present, the Petty Sessions

---

[61]   Judicature (NI) Act 1978, s 34(3). We note, for completeness, that the Court of Criminal Appeal was reconstituted by the Criminal Appeal (NI) Act 1968 with the same jurisdiction as before but in a more consolidated format.

[62]   *Courts in Northern Ireland: The Future Pattern* (Cmnd, 6892), para 24.

Service, the County Court Service and the staff of the Supreme Court, together with personnel from the Courts Administration Branch of the Northern Ireland Office.

iv) [T]he territorial reorganisation of courts in Northern Ireland; the county will no longer be the territorial basis for the jurisdiction of the inferior courts; instead, Petty Sessions districts will become coextensive with the new local government districts, and these districts will then be grouped together to form County Court circuits.[63]

In realising these purposes, the 1978 Act also gave effect to a carefully developed suite of recommendations concerning the organisation and jurisdiction of Northern Ireland's courts that had emerged from three judge-led reports.[64] As a result, the 1978 Act marks an enduring turning point in the development of the Court of Appeal.

Moreover, from the 1980s onwards, as part of the Supreme Court of Judicature the Court of Appeal ceased to apply rules descended from 'the old Irish courts' and instead adopted 'rules closely in line with the English rules of the supreme court'.[65] This had the benefit of enabling Northern Ireland practitioners

---

[63] These papers are accessible in the Public Records Office of Northern Ireland at NIO/9/2/2/12.

[64] See the *Report of the Committee on the Supreme Court of Judicature of Northern Ireland* (The MacDermott Report: Cmnd 4292, 1970); the *Report of the Joint Committee on Civil and Criminal Jurisdiction in Northern Ireland* (The Lowry Report: Cmnd 5431, 1972); and the *Report of the Committee on County Courts and Magistrates' Courts in Northern Ireland* (The Jones Report: Cmnd 5431, 1974).

[65] Carswell, n 58, 20. See the Rules of the Supreme Court (Northern Ireland) 1980, which were modelled closely on the English Rules of 1965. Under the Constitutional Reform Act 2005, Sch 11, para 3(1), the Rules may now be cited as the Rules of the Court of Judicature (Northern Ireland) (Revision) 1980.

to 'make use of the English White Book in arguing and deciding matters of procedure',[66] which obviously had the added benefit of making it generally less laborious for Northern Ireland judges to determine such points anew. However, the benefits of this procedural alignment did not last long, because the system in England and Wales underwent 'a fundamental change-over' to the Civil Procedure Rules in 1998 which was not (and still has not been) replicated in Northern Ireland.[67] While a useful text on the Northern Ireland specific practice and procedure of the Court was published by Barry Valentine in 1997 and supplemented with an addendum in 2000,[68] the most comprehensive annotations on the 1978 Act as later amended, and the Rules of the Court of Judicature made thereunder,[69] are now published by the same author in an online resource which is available only to Lexis+ subscribers.[70] It might be queried whether there is a good case to be made for revisiting this framework and the resources for navigating it, now that it is 46 years since the 1978 Act was passed. The judges we have interviewed hold different views about that proposal.[71]

---

[66] Ibid.

[67] Ibid.

[68] BJAC Valentine, *Civil Proceedings: The Supreme Court* (SLS Legal Publications (NI) 1997); BJAC Valentine, *Supplement to Civil Proceedings: The Supreme Court* (SLS Legal Publications (NI) 2000). Also see BJAC Valentine, *Criminal Procedure in Northern Ireland* (2nd edn, SLS Legal Publications (NI) 2010) Ch 15; BJAC Valentine, *Civil Proceedings: The County Court* (SLS Legal Publications (NI) 1999) Ch 20.

[69] Rules of the Court of Judicature (NI) 1980, available at www.justice-ni.gov.uk/publications/court-rules-publications, as amended up to June 2021. See Orders 59–61 in particular.

[70] See *Valentine: All Laws of Northern Ireland*, available to Lexis+ subscribers at https://plus.lexis.com/api/permalink/b4c756cb-3574-444b-9ca1-6450474bacf9/?context=1001073. This resource used to be distributed to subscribers by way of regularly updated CDs that were produced and sold by the Law Society of Northern Ireland, until it was bought over by Lexis+ in recent years.

[71] See Chapter 8.

We will not attempt to comment on all the provisions of the 1978 Act and the Rules of Court made thereunder, given that Valentine's commentaries are best consulted for those details. In general terms it may be helpful to conclude our discussion of the Act's effects with the following summary. The Court of Appeal is now a superior court of record which has inherited all the jurisdiction that was previously capable of being exercised by its 'general' predecessor and by the Court of Criminal Appeal which existed alongside that predecessor, as well as any other jurisdiction that is conferred upon it by the 1978 Act or any other statutory provisions.[72] It has no inherent or original jurisdiction, other than on certain ancillary and procedural matters,[73] but its statutory jurisdiction is vast. We cite the specific statutory basis for the most common civil and criminal appeal routes in Chapters 4 and 5 of this book, in the course of discussing cases that have been taken via each of those routes over the past 25 years.[74] At this stage we need only emphasise that while the Court generally hears no original applications, it is now burdened with a great deal of appellate work arising from its expansive statutory jurisdiction. Moreover, since 2005, the Lord/Lady Chief Justice has assumed a particularised responsibility for various statutory powers and duties flowing from his/her role as President of the Courts of Northern Ireland and Head of the Judiciary of Northern

---

[72] Judicature (NI) Act 1978, s 34(1)–(2).

[73] Valentine, *Civil Proceedings*, n 68, 491.

[74] We highlight, for completeness, that the Criminal Appeal (NI) Act 1980 consolidated various provisions; the Criminal Justice Act 1988 allowed 'references' to be made in relation to 'unduly lenient' sentences; the Criminal Appeal Act 1995 provided for possible miscarriages of justice to be referred by the Criminal Cases Review Commission, and the Criminal Justice (NI) Order 2004 permitted the prosecution to appeal against certain rulings by Crown Court judges.

Ireland.[75] Clearly, there are no longer any 'plum jobs' on the Court of Appeal.

2.4 Significant changes to the appointments process of the Court

The process for appointing judges to the Court of Appeal in Northern Ireland has changed in a number of ways since it was first established, though there has been relatively little written about those changes from an academic point of view.[76] In the next two sub-sections of this chapter, we will provide a synopsis of the most significant changes to the process that we have corroborated by studying original archival papers in the Public Records Office of Northern Ireland and in the National Archives.[77]

2.4.1 A politicised appointments system

The first set of judicial appointments to the Court of Appeal, discussed earlier, was made on an openly political basis. Formally, the relevant process initially involved the Prime Minister of Northern Ireland recommending individuals for

---

[75] Justice (NI) Act 2002, s 12, as amended by the Constitutional Reform Act 2005, s 11. The 2005 Act, s 59, renamed the Supreme Court of Judicature of Northern Ireland by removing the word 'Supreme'.

[76] We have read the draft of a discourse by Graham Truesdale, provisionally titled 'Doing the State Some Service: Judicial Appointments in Northern Ireland Since 1921', which fulsomely covers the history of senior judicial appointments in Northern Ireland. We trust that Truesdale's work will provide an insightful addition to the literature when it is published and we gratefully acknowledge the assistance that we have derived from it for the purposes of this chapter section.

[77] As indicated, this section focuses on how the appointments process has changed over time. See Appendix C for a full picture of how the composition of the Court has changed since its inception.

appointment to the UK Home Secretary, who would then decide on a final recommendation to the monarch.[78] However this practice was 'challenged' in 1945 when the Home Secretary decided to recommend that Samuel Porter, who was 'the father of the Bar' but did not belong to a political party, should be appointed to the Court of Appeal to replace the recently deceased Murphy LJ.[79] The Home Secretary recommended Porter's appointment despite the Prime Minister of Northern Ireland having recommended that William Lowry, the then Attorney General for Northern Ireland, should be appointed.[80] All of Lowry's Ulster Unionist predecessors in that role had been given judicial appointments,[81] but records show that the Home Secretary defended a departure from the conventional practice 'on two counts':

(a)   that the responsibility for advising the Crown rested with the Home Secretary alone and in the exercise of that responsibility he was not inhibited from seeking advice wherever he wished [and]

(b)   that in the past these appointments had invariably been made from one political party and the time had come to break this convention and to bring the whole field of the Bar under review.

---

[78]   There is an excellent historical summary of the appointment processes up to 1956 in a Ministerial advice letter dated 13 August 1956, in the Public Records Office of Northern Ireland at CAB/9/I/10/4.

[79]   The original correspondence about this episode is contained within the same file, ibid.

[80]   Ibid.

[81]   That is, Richard Best, Sir Anthony Babington, Edward Murphy, Arthur Black, and John Clarke MacDermott. It might be worth noting here that, as Claire Palley put it in 1972, active participation in politics is 'an accepted preliminary in many countries to the path of judicial preferment': 'The Evolution, Disintegration and Possible Reconstruction of the Northern Ireland Constitution' (1972) 1 *Anglo-American Law Review* 368, 398.

Despite initial resistance, the Prime Minister of Northern Ireland ultimately conceded that 'future holders of the office of Attorney General should have no claim, as of right, to succession to judicial office' and that the Home Secretary should 'aim to get the best and most suitable man, irrespective of his political views or of his occupancy of any particular political office, regard being had to the qualifications and merits of all the leading men at the Bar'.[82] Likewise, and notwithstanding spirited efforts to stress that 'constitutional proprieties demanded acceptance of the advice of the Prime Minister of the day', the Home Secretary prevailed in that it was eventually recognised 'there was no hope of re-affirming that principle'.[83]

The Home Secretary therefore controlled the process for judicial appointments to the Court of Appeal up until 1949, when another significant set of developments occurred. It was first proposed, in the context of a Bill which would become the Ireland Act 1949, that responsibility for the whole Supreme Court of Judicature of Northern Ireland should become a transferred matter.[84] This proposal was firmly rejected.[85] The then Lord Chief Justice, Sir James Andrews, wrote to the Prime Minister of Northern Ireland, Sir Basil Brooke, resisting the proposal with these words:

> I have had an opportunity of conferring separately (and, of course, in confidence) with all my colleagues on the Supreme Court bench in regard to the suggestion that the Supreme Court Service should cease to be 'Reserved', and should be transferred to the Government of Northern Ireland. ... I found that there was a complete unanimity of opinion against the change, viewed as it

---

[82] See n 78.

[83] Ibid.

[84] Ibid.

[85] Ibid.

was, entirely from the strictly legal standpoint. This confirms and strengthens my own opinion upon the matter. I think that, without any trace of personal egotism, I can claim that our Legal Service enjoys the confidence of the people of Northern Ireland: and I can see no sufficient reason for making a change which might gravely imperil our future, and for which I have never heard any public demand. The present system ensures independence which is vital.[86]

It was then suggested that 'the responsibility for making nominations to the Supreme Court Bench should be placed in the hands of the Lord Chancellor', which was ultimately agreed upon.[87] The procedure to be followed from late 1949 onwards was set out in a detailed memorandum on the 'Procedure for the Appointment of Lord [sic] Justices of Appeal in the Supreme Court of Judicature in Northern Ireland, and Judges of the High Court of Justice in Northern Ireland'.[88] The practical operationalisation of this procedure obviously involved an array of delicate political calculations, though for many years these were not a matter of public record. In 1992 one of us felt bound to write that it was 'impossible to say that a particular judge has ever been appointed because he was of a particular religion'.[89] It is clear from our more recent research based on subsequently disclosed papers that religion became a significant consideration for a certain period of time.

The single most illustrative example of religious discrimination in respect of a senior judicial appointment occurred in 1956.

---

[86] Ibid, letter dated 28 December 1948.

[87] n 78.

[88] An original copy of this memorandum is stored in a separate file in the Public Records Office of Northern Ireland: CAB/9/I/10/3.

[89] Brice Dickson, 'Northern Ireland's Troubles and the Judges' in Brigid Hadfield (ed), *Northern Ireland: Politics and the Constitution* (Open University Press 1992) 133.

In line with the process set out in the 1949 memorandum mentioned earlier, the then Lord Chief Justice, Lord MacDermott, listed a range of candidates whom he considered eligible for consideration by the Lord Chancellor, Lord Kilmuir, in respect of a vacancy created by the death of Porter LJ.[90] Cyril Nicholson QC was among those suggested by Lord MacDermott to Lord Kilmuir,[91] but 'secret' minutes of a meeting between these two reveal that Nicholson was apparently ruled out because 'it would be too difficult to appoint another Catholic to the Bench at present'.[92] This view was reinforced by a subsequent letter sent to Lord Kilmuir from the Prime Minister of Northern Ireland, Sir Basil Brooke, in which the latter stated that 'politically I couldn't support Cyril Nicholson as in my opinion it would unbalance the Judgeship and I would be open to very severe criticism'.[93] Shortly thereafter, in a 'confidential' letter from Lord MacDermott to Lord Kilmuir, the following admission was committed to page:

I went to the P.M. at Stormont last week to see if there was any possibility of him having second thoughts about C.A. Nicholson, Q.C. who on his own merits would rank high. Personally, the P.M. would have no objection to Nicholson but he felt that a second Roman Catholic in a Judiciary of five would be politically embarrassing, and on that account he could not acquiesce in his appointment.[94]

---

[90] Correspondence and minutes relating to this episode are accessible from the National Archives at LCO/2/8153 and from the Public Records Office of Northern Ireland at CAB/9/I/10/4.

[91] Ibid, LCO/2/8153, letter dated 21 July 1956, wherein Lord MacDermott stated, *inter alia*, that 'Mr. Nicholson is a Roman Catholic of good standing'.

[92] Ibid, LCO/2/8153, minutes dated 7 August 1956.

[93] Ibid, CAB/9/I/10/4, letter dated 5 September 1956.

[94] Ibid, LCO/2/8153, letter dated 11 September 1956.

Following these exchanges, Nicholson was not appointed.[95] Curran J was elevated to the Court of Appeal seat made vacant upon the death of Porter LJ and Herbert Andrew McVeigh QC was appointed to the High Court seat vacated by Curran J.

2.4.2 A gradually de-politicised appointments system

The weight laid upon the religious background of individual candidates for senior judicial positions seems to have reduced slowly over time. As such, by 1968 the Prime Minister of Northern Ireland, Terence O'Neill, was keen on avoiding so much as the appearance of religious preferment. In a letter to the UK Lord Chancellor, Lord Gardiner, which was copied to the UK Prime Minister, Harold Wilson, O'Neill set out the position as follows:

> Until the recent legislation authorising two additional appointments, our Supreme Court consisted of the Lord Chief Justice and four Judges. Traditionally, one of these five appointments had long been held by a Roman Catholic Judge. With the addition to the court of Mr. Justice McGonigle [sic] (at the same time as Mr. Justice Jones), the number of Roman Catholic Judges became two out of seven. The appointment now of Mr. Gibson in the place of Mr. Justice Sheil would reduce the ratio to one out of seven.
>
> It is distasteful to me to have to mention considerations which, in an ideal world, would be irrelevant. But we have learned from hard experience here that appointments made on merit alone are frequently criticised if they do not result in a balance between the two sections of our community.

---

[95] His son, Sir Michael Nicholson, was appointed to the High Court in 1986 and then to the Court of Appeal in 1995.

Moreover, the position of the Northern Ireland Government in relation to Supreme Court appointments is imperfectly understood, and if Mr. Justice Sheil is now replaced by a Protestant, I have no doubt that it will be insinuated, if not actually alleged, that it is the Northern Ireland Government which has brought its influence to bear to ensure the appointment of a Protestant.

You may well say that it is your duty to ignore this, and to appoint the person you consider best qualified. We have been in the same dilemma many times, and have made the same decision. But I do want to make it absolutely clear – although I hope you would in any case take it for granted – that we would be perfectly happy to see a qualified Roman Catholic barrister appointed to this vacancy.[96]

The Lord Chancellor responded in sympathetic terms:

I made a point of considering with Lord MacDermott the claims of the leading Roman Catholic Silks as well as a Roman Catholic county court Judge, but having done so I was left with no doubt at all that there is at present no other candidate as well qualified as Mr. Gibson. ... I am quite sure that in the long run there would be stronger criticism if I failed to recommend the man who is best qualified for appointment.[97]

The UK Prime Minister subsequently confirmed that 'if the appointment is criticised in the House of Commons I should certainly wish to make it clear that the Government here take full responsibility for the appointment and that it was made entirely on merits without pressure of any kind'.[98]

---

[96] CAB/9/I/10/4, letter dated 29 October 1968.

[97] Ibid, letter dated 30 October 1968.

[98] Ibid, letter dated 31 October 1968.

By 1984 there were still 'two Roman Catholic judges out of the nine judges of the Supreme Court' and records show that the religion of possible candidates was not taken into account by the Lord Chancellor 'unless, though this is not generally known, there were candidates of equal standing and ability and there was a serious imbalance in the Bench in favour of one side'.[99]

Eventually, the Lord/Lady Chief Justice was designated as the Head of the Judiciary of Northern Ireland[100] and a Northern Ireland Judicial Appointments Commission was created.[101] These changes were prompted by an extensive review of the criminal justice system that was carried out following the Belfast (Good Friday) Agreement of 1998.[102] That review recognised, *inter alia*, that 'the extent to which the composition of the judiciary reflects the society which it serves is a confidence issue and has implications for its legitimacy in the eyes of many in the community'.[103] The review further recognised that if there is 'a perception that judges come predominantly from a narrow pool, then there is liable to be concern that the way in which the law as a whole is developed will be unduly influenced by one particular set of values'.[104] These principles clearly informed the modern-day appointments system which resulted from the review.

The modern-day appointments system applicable to Northern Ireland judges at High Court level and below provides that appointments and recommendations for

---

[99] LCO/33/138, note by MD Heubner dated 25 June 1984.

[100] Justice (NI) Act 2002, s 12, as amended by the Constitutional Reform Act 2005, s 11.

[101] Justice (NI) Act 2002, ss 2 and 3, Schs 1 and 2; Justice (NI) Act 2004, ss 1 and 2, Sch 1.

[102] *Review of the Criminal Justice System in Northern Ireland* (HMSO, 30 March 2000) Ch 6.

[103] Ibid, para 6.85.

[104] Ibid.

appointment 'must be made solely on the basis of merit'[105] but still requires the relevant appointments commission to engage in a programme of action which, among other things, is 'designed to secure, so far as it is reasonably practicable to do so, that appointments to listed judicial offices are such that those holding such offices are reflective of the community in Northern Ireland'.[106] These rules may indirectly shape the pool of competitive candidates for the Court of Appeal. However, as regards the directly applicable rules for appointment to the office of Lord/Lady Chief Justice and as regards Lords/Ladies Justices of Appeal, the relevant legislation now in force simply requires the UK Prime Minister to consult both the incumbent Lord/Lady Chief Justice or, if they are unavailable, the senior Lord/Lady Justice of Appeal who is available, and the Northern Ireland Judicial Appointments Commission, before making a recommendation to the King.[107] In practice, the Prime Minister has 'asked the Chief Justice to establish a selection panel to make a recommendation for appointment' and it has been stated that all applications are considered strictly on the basis of merit.[108] The non-statutory criteria that applicants are expected to satisfy focus on 'legal skills'; 'personal

---

[105] On the concept of merit in this context, see John Morison, 'Finding "Merit" in Judicial Appointments: The Northern Ireland Judicial Appointments Commission (NIJAC) and the Search for a New Judiciary for Northern Ireland' in Anne-Marie McAlinden and Clare Dwyer (eds), *Criminal Justice in Transition: The Northern Ireland Context* (Hart Publishing 2015) Ch 7.

[106] Justice (NI) Act 2002, Sch 3, Pt 4, para 6.

[107] Judicature (NI) Act 1978, s 12, as amended by the Northern Ireland Act 2009, s 2 and Sch 2.

[108] See, for example, the following webpages announcing the launch of recruitment schemes for the post of Lord/Lady Justice of Appeal on 24 May 2019, 18 September 2020, and 13 May 2022: www.nijac.gov. uk/news/lord-or-lady-justice-appeal-court-appeal-northern-ireland-0; www.nijac.gov.uk/news/lord-or-lady-justice-appeal; www.nijac.gov.uk/ news/lord-or-lady-justice-appeal-court-appeal.

qualities'; 'understanding and fairness'; 'communication skills'; and 'leadership and management skills'.[109] The only statutory criterion for Court of Appeal appointments requires that applicants must be either a solicitor or a barrister of ten years' standing.[110] To this extent, there is an overtly apolitical emphasis to the modern-day appointments system.

2.5 Conclusion

In this chapter, we have sought to elucidate the steps by which the Court of Appeal first came into existence and to provide a guide to the most significant developments that have affected it since. In the first section, we described how the Court emerged consequent to the partition of Ireland and recounted some details about the first judges who were appointed to discharge its relatively small caseload. In the second section, we explained that while the legislative framework for the Court has been chopped and changed on several occasions, the modern-day Court has accumulated a vast statutory jurisdiction over both civil and criminal matters. In the third section, we delineated major modifications to the process for appointing Court of Appeal judges, including the notable shift from a highly politicised process, which included discrimination on the basis of religion, to a largely de-politicised one that places the principle of merit at its centre. Having provided this historical backdrop to the Court as it exists today, we can now turn to a more in-depth exploration of the Court's recent activities.

---

[109] Ibid.

[110] Judicature (NI) Act 1978, s 9, as amended by the Justice (NI) Act 2002, s 18(3).

THREE

An Overview of Recent Activities

3.1 Introduction

The Court of Appeal has existed for more than 100 years. While its core function remains the same today as in 1921, its workload and the way it has gone about dealing with it have changed considerably. To help paint the present picture, and to contextualise the qualitative analysis of the Court's civil and criminal jurisdiction in Chapters 4 and 5, this chapter summarises the activities of the Court during the past 25 years – essentially the period since the Belfast (Good Friday) Agreement of 1998. It first provides some statistical information on the number of cases disposed of by the Court, the number of 'sitting days', and the number of 'reported' cases. It then examines the part played by judges who have sat in the Court of Appeal, noting some interesting trends. Finally, particular attention is paid to several aspects of judgment-writing.

3.2 The Court's caseload

Table 3.1 displays the numbers of cases disposed of by the Court of Appeal during the past quarter of a century and also the numbers of reported cases, differentiating in each instance between civil cases and criminal cases.

It can be seen at a glance that the two jurisdictions have been almost equally demanding in terms of overall disposals, with 49 per cent of all disposals being criminal and 51 per cent civil, whereas the number of days when judges sit to

Table 3.1: Court of Appeal cases disposed of and reported, and sitting days, 1999–2023

Year	Civil disposals	Criminal disposals	All disposals	Sitting days (civil)	Sitting days (criminal)	Reported civil cases	Reported criminal cases	All reported cases
1999	69	53	122	143	92	19	6	25
2000	34	69	103	107	102	14	20	34
2001	74	67	141	190	129	27	28	55
2002	77	53	130	136	98	24	25	49
2003	79	57	136	81	86	20	34	54
2004	91	69	160	159	140	17	27	44
2005	106	87	193	220	195	23	32	55
2006	86	55	141	140	158	20	27	47
2007	91	51	142	83	57	33	21	54
2008	78	58	136	89	62	22	30	52
2009	84	65	149	114	53	442	21	65
2010	80	69	149	93	62	24	20	44
2011	91	63	154	102	61	31	38	69
2012	96	94	190	102	86	24	36	60

Table 3.1: Court of Appeal cases disposed of and reported, and sitting days, 1999–2023 (continued)

Year	Civil disposals	Criminal disposals	All disposals	Sitting days (civil)	Sitting days (criminal)	Reported civil cases	Reported criminal cases	All reported cases
2013	81	89	170	104	77	39	39	78
2014	97	96	193	111	85	44	37	81
2015	70	109	179	102	91	33	44	77
2016	92	91	183	134	80	34	24	58
2017	68	122	190	129	65	40	36	76
2018	79	104	183	111	83	25	26	51
2019	101	97	198	136	89	42	32	74
2020	79	77	156	88	86	30	30	60
2021	61	76	137	104	68	33	31	64
2022	95	95	190	149	69	39	29	68
2023	89	95	184	137	89	39	30	69
Total	2,048	1,961	4,009	3,064	2,263	740	723	1,463

The sources for disposals and sitting days are the annual *Judicial Statistics*, published jointly by the Northern Ireland Statistics and Research Agency and the Department of Justice: see www.justice-ni.gov.uk/publications/nicts-judicial-statistics (for 2008 to 2023). The sources for reported cases are the websites of the judiciary of Northern Ireland (www.judiciaryni.uk) and of the British and Irish Legal Information Institute (www.bailii.org).

hear criminal cases (42 per cent of the total) is generally lower than the number of days to hear civil cases (58 per cent).[1] This implies that, on average, civil cases are more complex than criminal cases and so take longer to hear. Regardless, the number of cases disposed of by the Court in recent years, whether civil or criminal, has fluctuated considerably since 1999. The average annual number of disposals during the first five-year period (1999 to 2003) was 126, while during the last five-year period (2019 to 2023) it was 173, an increase of 37 per cent.

Counter to expectations, the rise in the number of disposals has not been matched by a rise in the number of sitting days, whether in civil or criminal cases, and the number of sitting days spent on civil cases per year has remained consistently higher than the number spent on criminal cases. Only in two of the last 25 years were more days spent on criminal cases. Over the 25-year period the average number of days spent on civil cases was 123 while for criminal cases it was 91. During the first five-year period the averages were 131 and 101 days respectively, but during the final five-year period these were down to 123 and 80 days. The reduction is probably due in part to the impact of the COVID-19 pandemic in recent years but it is also likely to be attributable to more stringent judicial case management.

The total number of 'reported' cases during our period is 1,463, which is obviously a lot lower than the total number of disposals (4,009). A 'reported' case, in our definition, is one which is publicly available without any special request having to be made to the court for its release. They are published on the website of the Northern Ireland judiciary and the vast majority are also published on the website of

---

[1] A 'sitting day' is defined as 'a period of work by a judge in a single courtroom on a single day'. Different types of business might be heard at one sitting but business heard in different courtrooms is counted as separate sittings. Sittings held in judges' chambers are not included.

the British and Irish Legal Information Institute (BAILII).[2] A selection of concluded cases are not reported in this way because they are deemed to be relatively insignificant from a legal point of view, even though they may be very significant in the lives of the parties involved. The official statistics show that approximately two thirds of all criminal appeals are against sentence only and because they turn on the specific circumstances of each appellant they often do not have the requisite significance to deserve reporting. A very small number of appeals are, by the agreement of the parties, dealt with 'on the papers only'; that is, with no oral hearing. They too are rarely reported.[3]

Every appeal will result in a conclusion and on occasions this will be announced in what is called an *ex tempore* judgment spoken by the presiding judge at the end of the hearing, with reasons being given for the result. Generally speaking such judgments are not reported, though an audio version will be recorded in case a written transcription is requested. Indeed, one of the judges we spoke to for this project indicated that it is their preference 'to procure a transcript in every case for reasons of transparency'.[4] In all other cases, the appeal judges 'reserve' their judgment, which means that at some point after the court hearing they discuss what they think the result should be and decide which of them will write a judgment. The common practice today is that before the appeal even starts the Lady Chief Justice will designate which of the judges will be tasked with writing the eventual judgment, but of course this does not preclude one of the other judges in the case also writing a judgment, whether concurring or dissenting. Today, however, it is very unusual for there to be more than one judgment delivered: it did not happen at all during 2023, for instance.

---

[2] See the text accompanying Table 3.1.

[3] One example is *Horner v Cleaver Fulton and Rankin (a firm)* [2018] NICA 36.

[4] J5.

The standard practice is for the designated judgment-writer to produce a draft judgment, share it with his or her colleagues so that they can suggest any amendments to it, and then issue a revised judgment for delivery to the parties.

The presiding judge in each case typically 'signs off' a judgment when they submit it to the judges' librarian, who, subject to any minor amendments suggested to the judge and approved as corrections, then uploads it to the website of the Northern Ireland judiciary. We have been informed that in criminal cases where a decision is not published, it is often because a retrial has been ordered. Decisions on whether a case should be commercially reported by the Incorporated Council of Law Reporting for Northern Ireland are taken independently by that body, but the Court of Appeal in any given case can indicate whether it thinks a particular decision should be commercially reported when it is submitted to the judges' library. There are two commercially printed law report series in Northern Ireland: the *Northern Ireland Law Reports* and the *Northern Ireland Judgments Bulletin*. It is for the editors of those series to choose which cases on the judiciary's website should be included. Each of them provides more information about the case than the bare judgment on the judiciary's website: they name the barristers and solicitors involved in the case and in the *Northern Ireland Law Reports* there is a headnote which sums up the facts and the result of the case and also a list of previously reported cases referred to in the judgment. Each volume of these printed reports will contain perhaps 15 to 20 cases, so they represent well under one half of all the cases on the judiciary's website.

As Table 3.1 indicates, there are 1,463 reported Court of Appeal cases included on the website of the Northern Ireland judiciary and it is these upon which we have focused in the research for this book in order to illustrate the workings of the Court. Reported cases are by definition the most important from a legal point of view, they are freely accessible to everyone, and they are numerous enough to suggest that any findings we base on them are likely to hold good for unreported cases as well. More prosaically, it would have been extremely difficult (even if it had been permitted) for us to go through the Court files relating to the 2,546 unreported cases.

3.3 The composition of the Court

Since 1975 the Court of Appeal has consisted of four judges – the Lord or Lady Chief Justice (as its President) and three Lords Justices of Appeal (there has not yet been a Lady Justice of Appeal). During the 25-year period under review (1999 to 2023) a total of 20 different judges have occupied those positions.[5]

For almost the first six years – the first few years of Northern Ireland's peace process after the Belfast (Good Friday) Agreement – the composition of the Court of Appeal did not alter. The first change came in January 2004 when Sir Brian Kerr was appointed to replace Sir Robert Carswell as Lord Chief Justice, the latter having moved to the House of Lords as a Lord of Appeal in Ordinary. Kerr LCJ joined a Court on which the three Lords Justices were already well established in their positions: Sir Michael Nicholson had been a Lord Justice of Appeal since 1995,[6] Sir Liam McCollum since 1997,[7] and Sir Anthony Campbell since 1998[8] and they had all been appointed to the High Court bench before he had. The two

---

[5] See Appendix C for a picture of how the composition of the Court has changed since its inception.

[6] Sir Michael retired in 2006, after 11 years of service. He died on 30 October 2023, while this book was being written. For an obituary, which includes a reference to the religious discrimination his barrister father allegedly experienced when judicial preferments were occurring a generation earlier, see *The Irish Times*, 27 January 2024. For our account of the archival evidence substantiating that allegation, see Chapter 2.

[7] Sir Liam retired in the summer of 2004. He died on 5 June 2023.

[8] Sir Anthony retired in the summer of 2008, after ten years of service.

new Lords Justices appointed in 2007, Sir Malachy Higgins and Sir Paul Girvan, remained in post for seven and eight years respectively and after Sir Patrick Coghlin was appointed in 2008 he too remained for seven years. The most dominant player in our period, however, was Sir Declan Morgan, who was the Lord Chief Justice for just over 12 years, from 2009 to 2021. During that time he partnered with no fewer than 11 different Lords Justices, the last seven of whom served between 21 and 38 months only. The retirement age for judges was still 70 and time had caught up with them. Now that the retirement age has been raised again to 75 there is likely to be less of a turnover in Court of Appeal judges than in previous years.[9] It remains to be seen whether the periods served will come close to those served by some of the earliest Lords Justices: Sir James Andrews served from 1921 to 1937, Richard Best from 1925 to 1939, Arthur Black from 1949 to 1964, and Sir Lancelot Curran (the longest of all) from 1956 to 1975.

Recent years have also been momentous as regards the participation of female judges in the Court of Appeal. The first reported case in which a woman adjudicated there was *Harkin v Brendan Kearney and Company, Solicitors*, in which McBride J sat.[10] Madam Justice McBride was also the first woman to deliver a judgment in a reported Court of Appeal decision, in *R v Ruddy*.[11] Dame Siobhan Keegan, after becoming the first woman to be appointed as the Chief Justice of Northern Ireland in 2021, was thus also the first to preside in the Court of Appeal – *Re OV's (A Minor) Application* appears to be the first reported case in which that occurred.[12] We have also

---

[9] The retirement age was raised to 75 by the Public Service Pensions and Judicial Offices Act 2022, s 121 and Sch 1, in force from 10 March 2022.

[10] [2015] NICA 79.

[11] [2016] NICA 17.

[12] [2021] NICA 58.

witnessed the first reported case in which *two* female judges sat together in the Court of Appeal: *R v Hughes*.[13]

There are no *ex officio* members of the Court of Appeal in Northern Ireland, unlike in England and Wales. All members of the UK Supreme Court are *ex officio* members of the Court of Appeal of England and Wales if, at the date of their appointment, they were qualified for appointment as a Lord or Lady Justice of Appeal.[14]

3.3.1 The composition of appeal panels

It is the Lord or Lady Chief Justice who decides which judges should sit in any particular appeal. In *Re the Northern Ireland Human Rights Commission's Application* counsel objected to the fact that the composition of the Court of Appeal had been decided by Carswell LCJ, against whose decision the appeal in question was being brought. But the Court of Appeal rejected the point, McCollum LJ saying:

> I am not impressed by the suggestion that the Lord Chief Justice has been or could be thought to be influenced in any way by his perception of the likely attitude of any of the members of the court or that he would in any circumstances choose a court on the basis that it is one that would be likely to uphold his judgment irrespective of its assessment of the true merits of the case.[15]

---

13 [2022] NICA 12, a case in which guidance was given on the sentencing of persons who are found guilty of multiple incidents of domestic violence. We have learned that both McBride J and Keegan J, with Deeny LJ presiding, were to have sat in *Jordan's (Teresa) Application* [2018] NICA 23, but that prior to the hearing of the case on 1 May 2018 Keegan J was replaced by O'Hara J. Deeny LJ noted publicly at the time that it was the first occasion on which two female judges had sat in the Court of Appeal.

14 Senior Courts Act 1981, s 2(2)(c).

15 [2001] NICA 17, [2001] NI 271.

What is certainly clear is that the four judges who currently make up the Court of Appeal cannot by themselves cope with all the cases that are brought to the Court. In fact, this has been the position for quite some time. Table 3.2 indicates the various formations in which the Court sat in reported cases during the 20 years from 2004 to 2023.[16]

Three features stand out from Table 3.2. The first is that the number of cases which are dealt with only by the four permanent members of the Court of Appeal has dropped considerably. In the last five years (2019 to 2023) less than 20 per cent of the Court's decisions have been heard only by the Lord/Lady Chief Justice and the Lords Justices (and in 2023 the figure was just 4 per cent), whereas in the first five years (2004 to 2008) as many as 62 per cent were so heard. Over the entire 20-year period only 48 per cent of all cases were the sole preserve of the permanent members. The corollary of this development is that the Court has relied increasingly on High Court judges serving as *ad hoc* members of the Court of Appeal, as the Judicature (NI) Act 1978 permits.[17] In fact it is now the norm that a High Court judge will sit in a Court of Appeal case. In our interviews with judges who have sat on the Court of Appeal there was virtual unanimity that High Court judges benefited from the experience of serving in the Court of Appeal from time to time: it is a good opportunity for them to see how that Court goes about overseeing the work of judges in lower courts and it provides some training

---

[16] Reported cases dating from the first five years of our period (1999 to 2003) do not provide enough detail of the names of judges who sat in each case to enable accurate figures to be included in Table 3.2.

[17] Section 3(2) provides that 'Every judge of the High Court shall be a judge of the Court of Appeal for the purposes of its jurisdiction in a criminal cause or matter' and s 6(2) states that 'A judge of the High Court shall, if requested to do so by the Lord [or Lady] Chief Justice, sit and act as a judge of the Court of Appeal when that court is exercising jurisdiction other than jurisdiction in a criminal cause or matter'.

Table 3.2: The composition of appeal panels, 2004–23

Year	3-judge panels				2-judge panels		Total
	LCJ, LJ, and LJ	LJ, LJ, and LJ	LCJ/ LJ, LJ, and J	LCJ/ LJ, J, and J	LCJ/ LJ and LJ	LCJ/ LJ and J	
2004	24	4	14	0	0	0	42
2005	23	3	15	3	2	4	50
2006	20	8	13	2	3	0	46
2007	26	4	12	1	4	1	48
2008	28	4	10	0	4	0	46
2009	29	14	15	2	2	1	63
2010	22	10	7	0	4	0	43
2011	32	16	18	0	3	0	69
2012	33	8	16	0	2	0	59
2013	41	15	17	0	0	0	73
2014	29	11	35	1	2	0	78
2015	34	9	23	9	1	0	76
2016	16	12	19	4	5	2	58
2017	19	5	39	6	4	3	76
2018	10	7	16	2	12	3	50
2019	16	8	33	5	5	6	73
2020	10	5	25	9	5	5	59
2021	8	2	34	8	4	8	64
2022	13	1	24	8	8	13	67
2023	3	0	40	8	9	9	69
Total and %	436 36%	146 12%	425 35%	68 6%	79 6%	55 5%	1,209 100%

In some years it was not possible to determine how many judges sat in a number of the reported cases: 2004 (2), 2005 (5), 2006 (1), 2007 (6), 2008 (6), 2009 (2), 2010 (1), 2012 (1), 2013 (5), 2014 (3), 2015 (1), 2018 (1), 2019 (1), 2020 (1), and 2022 (1).

to those who may in due course apply for a permanent post in the Court of Appeal.[18]

The second noticeable feature of Table 3.2 is that much greater use is being made than before of *two* High Court judges in appeals. During the first ten-year period (2004 to 2013) the phenomenon occurred on only eight occasions, while in the second ten-year period (2014 to 2023) it occurred no fewer than 60 times. This is quite remarkable and can hardly be attributable to the need for High Court judges to learn about appellate processes because in those cases they will constitute the majority in the Court of Appeal and could out-vote the Chief Justice or Lord Justice who is presiding.[19] A closer look at these cases does not suggest that two High Court judges are being used more often in one kind of case rather than in another (for example, criminal rather than civil). It should be noted, as well, that the number of available High Court judges has increased over the years. Today there are 11 in office while in 2004 there were nine.

The third stand-out feature of Table 3.2 is the rise in the number of two-judge panels. Again, these are perfectly lawful because, while section 36(1) of the Judicature (NI) Act 1978 provides that 'every appeal to the Court of Appeal, other than an appeal under the Criminal Appeal Act, and every matter preliminary or incidental to such appeal shall be heard before three judges of that court', section 36(2) then provides that '[w]here the Lord [or Lady] Chief Justice so directs, any such appeal or matter may be heard before two judges'. The reference in section 36(1) is to the Criminal Appeal (NI) Act 1980, but it too contains a provision saying that, while every appeal or reference to the Court of Appeal under that

---

[18] See Chapter 8.

[19] In *Finucane v Secretary of State for Northern Ireland* [2017] NICA 7 Gillen LJ dissented from his two High Court colleagues, who held that on the facts the duty to conduct an investigation compliant with Art 2 of the ECHR had been revived.

Act must be heard before three judges, the Chief Justice may direct that any such appeal or reference or matter can be heard before two judges.[20] If two judges hear an appeal but cannot agree on the outcome, the case must be reheard before three judges if it is a criminal case and may be reheard before three judges if one of the parties to a civil case so applies.[21] It is interesting that in England and Wales a two-judge Court of Appeal is prohibited from determining, among other things, an appeal against conviction and an application to appeal to the Supreme Court.[22]

Table 3.2 shows that 11 per cent of appeals in the last 20 years have been heard by two-judge panels and in the last five years the figure has been 21 per cent. During the latter period 17 of the 69 two-judge appeals (25 per cent) were criminal appeals and in 40 appeals (58 per cent) one of the two judges was a High Court judge. We will return to this topic in more depth later in the book, where some differing points of view among the judges we interviewed will be set out.[23] For comparison's sake, we note at this juncture that in England and Wales three judges are the norm in both civil and criminal cases, although in the latter the three judges in question are usually one Lord/Lady Justice and either two High Court judges or one High Court and one circuit court judge.[24] The thinking there is that the involvement of judges who have experience

---

[20] Criminal Appeal (NI) Act 1980, s 44(1) and (2).

[21] Ibid, s 44(3) and Judicature (NI) Act 1978, s 36(3)(b).

[22] Senior Courts Act 1981, s 56(4). For some judicial reflections on the advantages and disadvantages of using two-judge courts in England and Wales, see Jack Beatson, Launcelot Henderson, and Keith Lindblom, 'Collective Judging in the Court of Appeal of England and Wales' in Birke Häcker and Wolfgang Ernst (eds), *Collective Judging in Comparative Perspective: Counting Votes and Weighing Opinions* (Intersentia 2020) 43–44.

[23] See Chapter 8.

[24] Penny Darbyshire, *Sitting in Judgment: The Working Lives of Judges* (Hart Publishing 2011) 324. A circuit court judge is more or less equivalent to a county court judge in Northern Ireland. The Senior Courts Act

of Crown Court trials can be very beneficial to the Court of Appeal. Appeals against sentence are routinely heard by two High Court judges in England and Wales, a practice which is unheard of in Northern Ireland. Legislation for Northern Ireland precludes the Court of Appeal from sitting as a bench of more than three judges, but the relevant legislation for England and Wales contains no such limitation.[25] Benches of five judges are used there in particularly important cases, especially on the criminal side.[26]

3.3.2 Assistance from retired judges and others

High Court and Court of Appeal judges who retire before the mandatory retirement age can be asked to sit as *ad hoc* judges in the Court of Appeal and this was fairly common during the 25-year period under review. There were times when some High Court positions were vacant for long periods, which meant that fewer of the serving High Court judges were available to sit in the Court of Appeal and greater resort was therefore had to retirees. It is difficult to give precise figures on the number of times retirees sat in cases because even though they are listed as a retiree when the judgment is published (by naming them, say, as Sir Paul Girvan rather than as Girvan LJ), it is often unclear whether the judge was already retired at the time the case was heard or whether the retirement occurred between the hearing and the delivery of the judgment. But there are many cases where it is certain that the judge was already retired when the case was heard. Sir Paul Girvan, who retired as a Court of Appeal judge in 2015, sat in at least 17

1981, s 55(6), precludes more than one circuit judge sitting in a Court of Appeal case in England and Wales.

[25] Contrast the Judicature (NI) Act 1978, s 36 with the Senior Courts Act 1981, ss 54 and 55.

[26] See Chapter 8 for some judicial reflections on the desirability of enabling this in Northern Ireland.

reported cases before he reached the age of 75 in 2023. Sir Richard McLaughlin, who retired as a High Court judge in 2012 at the age of 65, sat in at least 14 reported cases over the course of the subsequent ten years. There are cases where, by the time the judgment was delivered, all of the judges involved had retired.[27]

Serving Court of Appeal judges are now also helped in a different way – by a judicial assistant.[28] The introduction of this role was an initiative of the current Lady Chief Justice. In 2023 the Law Society of Northern Ireland, in conjunction with the Bar Council and the Lady Chief Justice's Office, advertised for a judicial assistant to directly support the Lady Chief Justice and the Court of Appeal.[29] According to the advertisement the role includes attending hearings and discussing relevant legal issues with the assigned judge, conducting research in connection with particular cases and preparing reports on particular points the judge would like to see addressed, proof-reading draft judgments, drafting press summaries under the direction of the Head of Judicial Communications in the Lady Chief Justice's Office, assisting with the assigned judge's extra-judicial communication and educational activities, and liaising with the Lady Chief Justice's Office and the Northern Ireland Courts and Tribunals Service with regard to cases and listings. The post was a short-term one (for ten months only) but the Law Society and Bar Council, who are paying for it, have already confirmed their support for a second post-holder.

---

[27] *Northern Ireland Electricity Networks Ltd v Brickkiln Waste Ltd* [2018] NICA 43; *Quinn v Cloughvalley Stores (NI) Ltd* [2019] NICA 5; *Walsh v Department of Justice* [2020] NICA 34.

[28] For the position in the Court of Appeal of England and Wales see Darbyshire, n 24, 325, and for the position in the UK Supreme Court see Alan Paterson, *Final Judgment: The Last Law Lords and the Supreme Court* (Hart Publishing 2013) 247–57.

[29] A second judicial assistant was recruited to support the High Court judge who has lead responsibility for judicial review applications.

There is also a Legal Unit within the Lady Chief Justice's Office. It employs a small number of experienced legally qualified staff on a full-time permanent basis, whose duties include assisting both the High Court and the Court of Appeal with their workload. We were told that in criminal appeals the Unit routinely summarises for the judges the arguments being raised. It also undertakes other specific research tasks at the request of individual judges.

3.3.3 A fourth Lord or Lady Justice of Appeal?

The figures presented in this section suggest that the workload of the Court of Appeal may exceed the capacity of the four permanent Court of Appeal judges to deal with alone. The size of the Court has not altered since 1975. The question can therefore fairly be asked: should a fourth post of Lord or Lady Justice of Appeal be created? There is power to do so within the Northern Ireland Executive's Department of Justice: with the agreement of the Northern Ireland Judicial Appointments Commission it can issue an order authorising the appointment of additional Lords or Ladies Justices of Appeal.[30] As far as we know, however, no serious consideration has yet been given to taking such a step, even though the evidence is mounting that such an investment could be easily justified. In England and Wales, which has a population roughly 31 times that of Northern Ireland, there are only 39 posts available for Lords and Ladies Justices of Appeal, so four in Northern Ireland might seem disproportionately high. That said, there must be some regard for the different practices in England and Wales that we have noted previously, including the routine use of two High Court judges in sentencing appeals. We will further explore judicial viewpoints on the proposal for a fourth Lord or Lady Justice of Appeal later in this book.[31]

---

[30] Judicature (NI) Act 1978, s 3(4).

[31] See Chapter 8.

3.4 The judges who delivered judgments

Our survey of reported decisions by the Court of Appeal since 1999 looked closely at which judges were delivering the judgments. The almost constant practice is for just one judgment to be delivered. Usually it is described as 'the judgment of the court', although occasionally it will be referred to more specifically as 'the judgment of the court to which all the judges have contributed'. Table 3.3 sets out the data relating to the 20 permanent members of the Court of Appeal who served during our 25-year period. Altogether they delivered 1,417 judgments. A further 150 (10 per cent of all judgments) were delivered by High Court judges.

The most telling figures in Table 3.3 are those in the right-most column. They indicate how frequently a judge in the Court of Appeal delivered a judgment. Clearly the most prolific judgment-writers tend to be the Chief Justices. During his tenure of that role Kerr LCJ gave a judgment in 84 per cent of the cases in which he sat, Morgan LCJ did so in 67 per cent of his cases, and Keegan LCJ has already done so in 77 per cent of hers. Had it been possible to determine the judgment rate for Carswell LCJ it is likely that the figure might have been even higher than Kerr LCJ's, since we do know that he gave a judgment in 76 per cent of *all* the reported cases between 1999 and 2003 (168 out of 217). Given that Chief Justices have so many other responsibilities besides serving as President of the Court of Appeal, it is astonishing that they are able to find the time to write as many appellate judgments as they do. Another very prolific judgment-writer, still in post, is McCloskey LJ, with a 76 per cent judgment rate. Furthermore, although they served as Lords Justices for relatively short periods, Stephens LJ and Deeny LJ also wrote judgments in at least half of the cases in which they sat. Girvan LJ, too, was very active in judgment-writing and over a much longer period.

Of course, such statistics can both reveal and conceal certain insights. We have been informed, for example, that while the number of reported judgments issued by Campbell

Table 3.3: Judgments issued by permanent members of the Court of Appeal, 1999–2023*

Name of judge	Time served on the Court of Appeal	Number of reported cases in which the judge sat**	Number of judgments issued	Percentage of cases in which a judgment was given
Carswell LCJ	5 years	n/a	168	n/a
Nicholson LJ	8 years	n/a	70	n/a
McCollum LJ	5 years, 8 months	n/a	14	n/a
Campbell LJ	10 years	n/a	35	n/a
Kerr LCJ	5 years, 5 months	193	162	84%
Sheil LJ	2 years, 2 months	76	8	11%
Higgins LJ	7 years, 5 months	285	46	16%
Girvan LJ	8 years, 8 months	333	144	43%
Coghlin LJ	7 years	265	64	24%
Morgan LCJ	12 years, 2 months	471	317	67%
Gillen LJ	3 years, 3 months	140	45	36%
Weatherup LJ	2 years	83	27	33%
Weir LJ	2 years	89	23	26%
Stephens LJ	3 years, 1 month	109	54	50%
Deeny LJ	2 years	58	24	41%
Treacy LJ	6 years, 2 months	169	53	31%
McCloskey LJ	4 years, 4 months	120	91	76%

Table 3.3: Judgments issued by permanent members of the Court of Appeal, 1999–2023* (continued)

Name of judge	Time served on the Court of Appeal	Number of reported cases in which the judge sat**	Number of judgments issued	Percentage of cases in which a judgment was given
Maguire LJ	1 year, 8 months	53	7	13%
Keegan LCJ	2 years, 4 months	82	63	77%
Horner LJ	1 year, 4 months	35	2	6%
Total	n/a	n/a	1,417	n/a

* The column on 'judgments issued' includes judgments delivered after the judge's retirement as a member of the Court of Appeal but not those issued while he or she was still a High Court judge. ** Of necessity these figures exclude cases where it has not been possible to determine the full composition of the Court (see n 16).

LJ (35) might look surprisingly low for a Lord Justice of Appeal who was in post for ten years, he 'was an influential member of the Court of Appeal in that he would be relied on when it came to the formulation of decisions'.[32] Thus, by virtue of this influential position, it has been suggested to us that Campbell LJ may have sat more often with the Lord Chief Justice in 'weighty' cases, where he would make substantial contributions which cannot be reflected in Table 3.3.[33]

3.4.1 Concurring and dissenting judgments

Unlike in England and Wales there is no legislation in Northern Ireland requiring only a single judgment to be given in a Court

---

[32] J6.
[33] J6.

of Appeal case unless the presiding judge is of the opinion that 'the question is one of law on which it is convenient that separate judgments should be pronounced'.[34] The reality is, however, that in Northern Ireland both concurring and dissenting judgments are extremely rare. The Court of Appeal almost always speaks univocally.

Throughout the 25-year period under review, during which there were 1,463 reported cases, single concurring judgments were delivered in only 24 cases and two concurring judgments in only 11. That means that concurring judgments were given in just 2.4 per cent of all cases. As regards dissenting judgments (whether full or partial), there were just 26 (1.8 per cent). In seven of those cases there was a further appeal to the House of Lords or Supreme Court.

3.4.2 The approach to precedents

The Court of Appeal in Northern Ireland is bound by decisions of the House of Lords and the Supreme Court, unless those precedents are not directly relevant because they turn on the wording of legislation which is not applicable in Northern Ireland.[35] The Court of Appeal also generally follows its own previous decisions, as McCloskey LJ confirmed in *Doherty v Ministry of Defence*,[36] where he said:

> There is a strong general principle that the Court of Appeal in this jurisdiction is bound by its previous decisions. Our approach essentially mirrors that of the English Court of Appeal dating from *Young v*

---

[34] Senior Courts Act 1981, s 59.

[35] *Re RM's Application* [2022] NICA 35, [2003] NI 274. The test in question related to when it is lawful to detain a mentally ill person in hospital for treatment. The Supreme Court later reversed the Court of Appeal's decision: [2024] UKSC 7, [2024] 1 WLR 1280.

[36] [2020] NICA 9, [2021] NIJB 193, [30].

Bristol Aeroplane. ...[37] The two leading decisions in this jurisdiction are *Leppington v Belfast Corporation* ...[38] and, more recently, *Re Rice's Application.*[39]

As regards previous decisions by the Court of Appeal in England and Wales, these are seen as persuasive but not binding in Northern Ireland. The relevant principle was confirmed by Campbell LJ in *Re Staritt's and Cartwright's Applications*:

> It has been long established that while this court is not technically bound by decisions of courts of corresponding jurisdiction in the rest of the United Kingdom it is customary for it to follow them to make for uniformity where the same statutory provision or rule of common law is to be applied. ...[40] This is not to say that the court will follow blindly a decision that it considers to be erroneous.[41]

The Court of Appeal in Northern Ireland is also willing to treat decisions by the Inner House of the Court of Session in Scotland as persuasive.[42] In addition, the Court has occasionally

---

[37] [1944] KB 718, 729–30, per Lord Greene MR.

[38] DR Miers, 'Rotten Eggs in the Court of Appeal' (1969) 20 *NILQ* 308. In *Leppington* Lord MacDermott CJ suggested that the Court of Appeal in Northern Ireland should be allowed to depart from a previous decision if it felt that its *ratio* was unclear.

[39] [1998] NI 265.

[40] Here Campbell LJ cited *McCartan v Belfast Harbour Commissioners* [1910] 2 IR 470, 494; *Re Northern Ireland Road Transport Board and Century Insurance* [1941] NI 77, 107; *Income Tax Commissioners v Gibbs* [1942] AC 402, 414 and *McGuigan v Pollock* [1955] NI 74, 106.

[41] [2005] NICA 48, [2006] NIJB 249, [21]. See too Morgan LCJ in *SH v RD* [2013] NICA 44, citing *Beaufort Development v Gilbert Ash* [1997] NI 142; also see *Baranowski v Rice* [2014] NIQB 122, [19], per Stephens J, citing yet further authorities.

[42] See *Re Meehan's Application* [2018] NICA 42, [2020] NI 440, [38], where the Court did not demur from Sir Paul Girvan's statement at first instance

taken into account judgments issued by the Irish Court of Appeal and the Irish Supreme Court.[43]

The Court of Appeal's invocation of both binding and non-binding precedents is an essential part of how it manages to achieve a good measure of consistency and efficiency when dealing with similar points of law and fact in the course of dispatching its large caseload. It is clearly aware of the conceptual tension associated with the doctrine of precedent; namely, 'a tension between, on the one hand, the certainty and predictability we need to satisfy the rule of law and achieve systemic justice, and, on the other hand, our perfectly proper concern over achieving justice in the individual cases'.[44] As Lord Denning put it to his fellow Law Lords in 1959, the doctrine of precedent 'does not compel your Lordships to follow the wrong path until you fall over the edge of a cliff'.[45]

3.5 Conclusion

This chapter has tried to convey a general sense of the quantity of work which the Court of Appeal has undertaken over the past 25 years. Among other features it has highlighted are the

---

that the Court of Appeal should 'follow and apply the ratio of decisions of the Inner House where the law in the two jurisdictions was essentially the same'.

[43] See, for example, *Quinn v Cloughvalley Stores (NI) Ltd* [2019] NICA 5, [38], citing *The Governor and Company of the Bank of Ireland v Brian O'Donnell* [2015] IECA 73, [2016] 2 IR 185; *Department of Finance v Quinn* [2019] NICA 41, [2021] NI 1, [24], citing *National Asset Management Agency v Commissioner for Environmental Information* [2015] IESC 51, [2015] 4 IR 626.

[44] Robert J Sharpe, *Good Judgment: Making Judicial Decisions* (University of Toronto Press 2018) 168.

[45] *Ostime (Inspector of Taxes) v Australian Mutual Provident Society* [1960] AC 459, 489; cited in ibid.

increasing reliance on High Court judges and the dominant role played by the Chief Justice. The following two chapters look more closely at the way the Court has conducted itself in relation first to its civil jurisdiction and then to its criminal jurisdiction.

FOUR

Civil Business

4.1 Introduction

This chapter opens with a statistical overview of the types of reported civil appeals dealt with by the Court of Appeal during the past 25 years. It then engages in a qualitative analysis of the key types of civil appeals, beginning with appeals from the High Court, where the absence of a general requirement for leave is highlighted. A more specific section follows on appeals from the High Court in judicial review cases. Finally, we touch upon appeals from courts and tribunals by way of case stated or otherwise on points of law only. A preliminary point is that, in civil cases especially (because in criminal cases legal aid will usually cover the costs), the expense involved in bringing an appeal is far from negligible. In 2024, regardless of the nature or size of the sums at issue, the fee payable on the filing of a notice of appeal or case stated is £711. If the respondent wishes to contend on the appeal that the decision of the court below should be varied in any way, or that it was wrong in whole or in part, the fee payable is £533. And if lawyers are instructed, their fees will of course add to the overall cost of pursuing an appeal. As far as we know no empirical research has yet been conducted on what impact the level of fees is having on access to the Court of Appeal.

4.2 Types of civil appeals

As we indicated in Chapter 3, during the period 1999 to 2023 there were almost identical numbers of civil and criminal cases reported: 740 of the former and 723 of the latter. Likewise, the percentage of cases disposed of that were reported was almost identical for both civil and criminal cases (36 per cent and 37 per cent, respectively). But many more sitting days were devoted to civil cases than to criminal cases (58 per cent as opposed to 42 per cent). At the appeal level civil cases simply require more court time than criminal cases.

Civil appeals are also more varied than criminal appeals. The criminal law is a relatively small and discrete area of law while civil law ranges far and wide over all other aspects of societal life. The array of courts and other bodies from which appeals can be brought to the Court of Appeal on civil law issues is therefore much greater than it is on criminal law issues. For present purposes we will divide that array into two categories: (1) the High Court and (2) inferior courts, tribunals, and other bodies. Table 4.1 gives a breakdown of the number of reported cases within each of those categories over the past 25 years.

The lion's share of civil appeals (76 per cent) clearly derives from the High Court. The fact that High Court judges also commonly sit as judges in the Court of Appeal means that those individuals are, in effect, regularly marking their colleagues' homework. This is accepted practice and does not seem to cause any difficulties. On the contrary, it helps to make High Court judges more aware of what the Court of Appeal expects from the lower court.

4.3 Appeals from the High Court in general

Appeals can normally be taken to the Court of Appeal from any High Court decision, but legislation specifies three types of decision from which an appeal can be taken only if leave has first been granted by the High Court and a further nine types of situations where an appeal is prohibited altogether.[1] Appeals

---

[1] Judicature (NI) Act 1978, s 35(2). Procedures to be followed in appeals from the High Court are laid down in Order 59 of the Rules of the Court of Judicature (NI) 1980 (hereafter 'RCJ (NI) 1980').

Table 4.1: The source of civil appeals, 1999–2023

Source of appeal	Number of reported cases
High Court	**566**
High Court judges	563
High Court Masters	3
Inferior courts	**20**
Magistrates' courts	6
County courts	14
Tribunals and other bodies	**154**
Industrial Tribunal	93
Fair Employment Tribunal	18
Social Security Commissioner	16
Child Support Commissioner	1
Social Security Appeal Tribunal	1
Pensions Ombudsman	3
Upper Tribunal	9
Immigration (and Asylum) Tribunal	3
Lands Tribunal	8
Northern Ireland Valuation Tribunal	1
Enforcement of Judgments Office	1
Total	**740**

are in some instances banned under the common law too.[2] The three situations in which leave is required are where the High Court has made an order with the consent of the parties or as to costs only, where (with some exceptions[3]) the High Court has issued an interlocutory order or judgment,[4] and where the

---

[2] See the list of eight common law prohibitions in the *Review Group's Report on Civil Justice* (2017), available at www.judiciaryni.uk/publicati ons/review-groups-report-civil-justice, App 7. For an example of leave to appeal being refused because the issue at question was 'academic', see *Re Bryson's Application* [2022] NICA 38.

[3] For example, where the liberty of the subject or contact with minors is involved.

[4] This is the case whether the High Court order or judgment was a first instance decision or in an appeal from a Master: *Rodgers v Rodgers* [2022] NICA 26.

High Court has made a decision under the Insolvency (NI) Order 1989.[5] It is relatively unusual for a Court of Appeal in a common law jurisdiction to have such limited control over its own caseload, although the Court of Appeal in the Republic of Ireland is in the same position.[6]

4.3.1 The leave requirement

In the 2017 Report of the Review Group on Civil Justice, chaired by Gillen LJ, careful consideration was given to the issue of leave in civil appeals. In the end it recommended that leave to appeal should be required in every appeal to the Court of Appeal. Applications for leave should be determined on the papers by one judge, but if leave is refused the party aggrieved should then be able to proceed to an oral hearing, again before a single judge. Thereafter there should be no right of appeal against a grant or refusal of leave.[7] Underlying this recommendation was the belief that the current system wastes valuable judicial time, as is made clear in the Review's introductory chapter:

> there is an unnecessary premium on an extensive oral process in the appeal system in many cases that are wholly unmeritorious. The result is an unnecessary and disproportionate waste of time and expense. Accordingly, we have recommended alterations to the granting of leave mechanism and the appeal thresholds. In addition, consideration is given to ADR [Alternative Dispute Resolution], unnecessary proliferation of documentation, a re-examination of costs, non-compliance with directions and hearing management in appeal hearings.[8]

---

[5] Judicature (NI) Act, s 35(2)(f), (g), and (j).

[6] Courts (Supplemental Provisions) Act 1961 (Ireland), s 7A, inserted by the Court of Appeal Act 2014 (Ireland), s 8.

[7] n 2, paras 15.29–15.33 and Recommendations CJ114 to CJ 117 (p 225).

[8] Ibid, 5, para 1.19.

The Gillen Review's recommendation has not to date been implemented and, as Chapter 8 will show, there are conflicting views among current and recently retired judges as to the desirability of introducing a leave stage for all High Court cases.

4.3.2 The test for leave, when required

Closely related to whether leave should be required is the question of what test should be applied by the Court of Appeal if it is required. The current position is reflected in the following quotation from a judgment delivered by Treacy LJ in 2022:

> Leave to appeal will be granted if there is a prima facie case of error; or a question of general principle not already decided; or a question of importance upon which further argument and a decision of the Court of Appeal would be to the public advantage. ...[9] In cases not involving a point of general principle or public advantage, the appellant must show 'an arguable case with a reasonable prospect of success that the trial judge had gone plainly wrong'. ...[10] This is the test that must be applied whether leave is being sought from the High Court or on renewal of an application for leave to the Court of Appeal.[11]

The test mentioned is already a broad one, but on occasions the Court of Appeal has gone even further. In *Re McNamee and McDonnell's Application* it accepted that there may be cases where there is a compelling reason to give permission

---

[9] Here the judge cited *Supreme Court Practice* (1999), at 59/14/18. This is the so-called 'White Book'; that is, the 'bible' of civil procedure in England and Wales.

[10] Here the judge cited *Flynn v Chief Constable of the PSNI* [2018] NICA 3, [2020] NI 293.

[11] *Department of Finance, Land and Property Services v Foster* [2022] NICA 19, [9]. See too *Moffatt v Moffatt* [2015] NICA 61, per Gillen LJ.

to appeal despite the fact that the usual test is not met.[12] As support for this position Morgan LCJ cited a 1997 Practice Note issued by Lord Woolf MR for England and Wales, where he stated that:

> There can be many reasons for granting leave even if the court is not satisfied that the appeal has any prospect of success. For example, the issue may be one which the court considers should in the public interest be examined by this court or, to be more specific, this court may take the view that the case raises an issue where the law requires clarifying.[13]

The example provided by Lord Woolf is perhaps not a helpful one, since what is in the 'public interest' is likely to also be to the 'public advantage', a criterion already mentioned in the usual test. Indeed, rather than suggesting that the current test is too narrow one might more validly argue that it is too wide – so much so as to be almost meaningless.

That was the prompt behind the Gillen Review's proposal that the test should be tightened. At one point the Review seems to favour the test that is already applied for appeals from a county court, a family court, or the High Court to the Court of Appeal in England and Wales; namely, that the appeal raises an important point of principle or practice or that there is some other compelling reason for the Court of Appeal to hear the appeal.[14] But in its list of recommendations the Review states that if this test is not implemented 'as a universal threshold' then for all appeals to the Court of Appeal from tribunals,

---

[12] [2011] NICA 40. This wider approach seems to have been re-approved, although not applied on the facts of the case, in *JP Murphy Ltd v Downey* [2022] NICA 25.

[13] *Smith v Cosworth Casting Processes Ltd (Practice Note)* [1997] 1 WLR 1538.

[14] n 2, para 15.35. The test in England and Wales is provided for by the Access to Justice Act 1999, s 55(1). It is also the test already used for

magistrates' courts, and county courts there should at least be a requirement that they be brought by a notice of appeal that states the questions of law on which the appeal is founded.[15] Moreover, in appeals from the High Court on interlocutory matters as well as in substantive appeals by way of 're-hearing' the threshold for granting leave should be raised to 'a real prospect of success' or 'some other compelling reason' for the Court of Appeal to hear the appeal.[16] As yet, however, these recommendations remain unimplemented.

If the High Court refuses leave in a case where it is required, the Court of Appeal can itself grant leave only if it has statutory authority to do so. This was made clear in *Re McShane's Application*, where a High Court judge refused leave to appeal against a decision by the Northern Ireland Local Government Commissioner for Standards that a local councillor should be suspended for three months.[17]

If any person or organisation wishes to intervene in an appeal they have to seek the permission of the Court. Applications to intervene are fairly common in judicial review cases, but the Court of Appeal will expect the intervener to have a special remit or expertise in the subject matter of the case and it will usually not want the intervener to duplicate arguments already being put forward by a party in the case. At times the Court might question whether a statutory organisation has the legal right to intervene. In 2001 the Court of Appeal in Northern Ireland held, by a majority, that the Northern Ireland Human Rights Commission had no right to intervene in an inquest in

---

appeals from the Upper Tribunal to either the Court of Appeal in England and Wales or the Court of Appeal in Northern Ireland: see the Appeals from the Upper Tribunal to the Court of Appeal Order 2008, art 2.

[15] Ibid, para 15.40 and Recommendation CJ 119 (p 225).
[16] Ibid, para 15.41 and Recommendation CJ120 (p 225).
[17] [2009] NICA 69. The long-standing precedent for this approach is *Lane v Esdaile* [1891] AC 210.

order to put forward human rights arguments,[18] but the House of Lords overturned that decision.[19]

4.3.3 Time limits for appeals

The Court of Appeal adopts quite a strict approach to deadlines relating to civil appeals. This is usually six weeks from the date on which the judgment or order of the court below was filed.[20] On numerous occasions in the past 25 years the Court has been asked to extend the time limit. The approach to be applied was clearly set out by Lord Lowry as far back as 1979:

> Where a time-limit is imposed by statute it cannot be extended unless that or another statute contains a dispensing power. Where the time is imposed by rules of court which embody a dispensing power … the court must exercise its discretion in each case, and for that purpose the relevant principles are:
>
> (1) whether the time is sped: a court will, where the reason is a good one, look more favourably on an application made before the time is up,
> (2) when the time-limit has expired, the extent to which the party applying is in default,
> (3) the effect on the opposite party of granting the application and, in particular, whether he can be compensated by costs,
> (4) whether a hearing on the merits has taken place or would be denied by refusing an extension,

---

[18] *Re Northern Ireland Human Rights Commission's Application for Judicial Review* [2001] NICA 17, [2001] NI 271 (Kerr J dissenting).

[19] *In re Northern Ireland Human Rights Commission* [2002] UKHL 25, [2002] NI 236 (Lord Hobhouse dissenting).

[20] RCJ (NI) 1980, Order 59, r 4. If the appeal is from an interlocutory order the time limit is 21 days.

(5) whether there is a point of substance (which in effect means a legal point of substance when dealing with cases stated) to be made which could not otherwise be put forward, and

(6) whether the point is of general, and not merely particular, significance.[21]

In 2017 the Civil Justice Review recommended that applications to appeal out of time should, like applications for leave to appeal, be dealt with by a single judge, with the applicant having the right to an oral hearing before a single judge if the extension of time is refused on the papers alone. But the Review went on to suggest, 'to ensure the principle of fairness prevails', that if a single judge does not grant the extension even after an oral hearing the applicant should then be able to have the matter considered by a full Court of Appeal.[22] There is merit in such a proposal because it should reduce the amount of judicial time wasted on hopeless applications, but the fact remains that, whatever number of judges considers the application it will always be necessary – bearing in mind the fifth and sixth of Lord Lowry's relevant principles – for the court to examine in some detail the merits of the points being raised in the proposed appeal. We shall see in the next chapter that the same problem commonly arises in criminal appeals.

4.3.4 The approach to facts and inferences

The Court of Appeal's general approach to civil appeals has been reaffirmed many times and appears to be identical to that

---

[21] *Davis v Northern Ireland Carriers* [1979] NI 19. For a typical example of this precedent being applied, see *Walsh v Office of the Industrial Tribunals* [2021] NICA 26.

[22] n 2, paras 15.43–15.44 and Recommendations CJ121 and CJ122 (pp 225–6).

adopted by the Court of Appeal in England and Wales. It was summed up most recently by McCloskey LJ in *Kerr v Jamison*:[23]

> Where invited to review findings of primary fact or inferences the appellate court will attribute weight to the consideration that the trial judge was able to hear and see a witness and was thus advantaged in matters such as assessment of demeanour, consistency and credibility. ...[24] The review of the appellate court is more extensive where findings are made at first instance on the basis of documentary and/or real evidence. However even where the primary facts are disputed the appellate court will not overturn the judge's findings and conclusions merely because it might have decided differently. ...[25] The deference of the appellate court will of course be less appropriate where it can be demonstrated that the first instance judge misunderstood or misapplied the facts.[26]

The UK Supreme Court seems to approve of this approach too, with Lord Kerr's judgment in *DB v Chief Constable of the Police Service of Northern Ireland* now commonly cited as the main authority on the matter.[27] There Lord Kerr said that

---

[23] [2019] NICA 48, [35]. This case was itself cited with approval by Humphreys J in *Holchem Laboratories Ltd v Henry* [2021] NICA 35, [25]. See too Morgan LCJ in *Heaney v McEvoy* [2018] NICA 4, [17]–[19], which McCloskey J endorsed in *Herron v Bank of Scotland plc* [2018] NICA 11, [24].

[24] Here the judge cited *Kitson v Black* [1976] 1 NIJB, 5–7.

[25] Here the judge cited *White v Department of the Environment* [1988] 5 NIJB 1.

[26] Here the judge cited *Northern Ireland Railways v Tweed* [1982] 15 NIJB, [10]–[11].

[27] [2017] UKSC 7, [2017] NI 301. But see too Lord Reed in *Henderson v Foxworth Investment Ltd* [2014] UKSC 41, [2014] 1 WLR 2600, [67], cited by Lord Hodge in *Carlyle v Royal Bank of Scotland* [2015] UKSC 13, 2015 SC (UKSC) 93, [21]–[22], who in turn was cited by Gillen LJ in *H v H* [2015] NICA 77, [25]: 'It follows that, in the absence of

in the case before him, which was about whether the police had misunderstood their powers in relation to unauthorised parades, 'the Court of Appeal should have evinced a greater reluctance in reversing the judge's findings than they appear to have done'. He added:

> Impressions formed by a judge approaching the matter for the first time may be more reliable than a concentration on the inevitable attack on the validity of conclusions that he or she has reached which is a feature of an appeal founded on a challenge to factual findings. The case for reticence on the part of the appellate court, while perhaps not as strong in a case where no oral evidence has been given, remains cogent.[28]

Fresh evidence is admissible in civil appeals, but there is no test of 'necessary or expedient in the interests of justice' as there is in criminal appeals.[29] According to rules of court, new evidence is admissible in civil cases if (a) it could not with reasonable diligence have been obtained for the trial, (b) it would probably have had an important influence on the outcome of the trial, and (c) it appears credible.[30]

A similar approach is adopted when attempts are made to appeal on grounds that were not even considered by the judge

---

some other identifiable error, such as (without attempting an exhaustive account) a material error of law, or the making of a critical finding of fact which has no basis in the evidence, or a demonstrable misunderstanding of relevant evidence, or a demonstrable failure to consider the relevant evidence, an appellate court will interfere with the findings of fact made by a trial judge only if it is satisfied that his decision cannot reasonably be explained or justified.'

[28] Ibid, [80].

[29] See Chapter 5.

[30] RCJ (NI) 1980, Order 59, r 10(2). These are the criteria set out by the Court of Appeal in England and Wales in *Ladd v Marshall* [1954] 1 WLR 1489.

at first instance. In *Kelly v Prison Service of Northern Ireland* Stephens LJ, as he then was, followed the position in England and Wales on this point.[31] This means that three conditions again need to be satisfied before new issues can be raised at the appellate level: the other party (a) must have had adequate opportunity to deal with the point, (b) must not have acted to his or her detriment on the faith of the earlier omission to raise the point, and (c) must be adequately protected in costs.[32]

4.3.5 Criticisms of lawyers and judges

The Court of Appeal recently issued a stern rebuke to lawyers who do not prepare for an appeal in the prescribed way. In *Taylor v Department for Communities* the appellant was appealing against a High Court ruling that his housing benefit payments should be suspended while he was in prison. The Court of Appeal said that the appeal would be struck out unless the 'multiple failings' in the appellant's case, especially his breach of the duty of candour, were fully rectified within ten days. Not mincing his words, McCloskey LJ characterised the lawyers' Notice of Appeal thus:

> It cannot be said that the Notice of Appeal ... is unduly informative or intelligible. Disappointingly, it is precisely the opposite. The grounds of appeal are of the 'boilerplate', diffuse and opaque variety so frequently deprecated by this court. There are eight grounds in total. Each of them recites that the judge '... erred in law by his conclusion that ...', without accompanying specificity or particularisation. Grounds of appeal couched in terms of this kind are simply meaningless.[33]

---

[31] [2019] NICA 25.

[32] These conditions were laid down by Nourse LJ in *Pittalis v Grant* [1989] QB 605 and approved by the Court of Appeal in England and Wales in *R (Humphreys) v Parking and Traffic* [2017] RTR 22.

[33] [2022] NICA 8, [13].

Even more worryingly, the judge added a note observing that '[i]n a very recent exercise of judicial scrutiny of all live civil appeals in the Court of Appeal system, around 40 cases in total, the diagnosis was that the Notice of Appeal was defective in every case. Not one passed muster.'[34]

The Civil Justice Review highlighted the problems of lawyers burdening the Court of Appeal with unnecessary or late documents and not complying with judicial directions.[35] It consequently made recommendations that in such instances solicitors and even legally aided litigants should be penalised as regards costs.[36] It also observed that when leave is required for an appeal the parties should be reminded that they have the option of seeking a mediated solution to their dispute, as occurred when the Bar Council brought a judicial review application against the Department of Justice relating to rises in legal aid rates.[37]

There are also examples of cases where the judge in the lower court made mistakes. In one case a judge was said to have given inaccurate advice to a litigant on his appeal rights[38] while in another a judge was criticised for asking lawyers to develop submissions based on ECHR case law but then not dealing with those arguments in his judgment.[39] A coroner has also been rebuked for giving the impression that he was biased in favour of a particular outcome while conducting an inquest.[40] All three of those cases were decided as recently as 2022.

---

[34] Ibid.

[35] n 2, paras 5.49–5.52.

[36] Ibid, Recommendations CJ127 to CJ131 (p 226).

[37] Ibid, para 15.47 and Recommendation CJ126 (p 226). See 'Long-running legal aid dispute resolved' (*The Belfast Telegraph*, 11 February 2016), www. belfasttelegraph.co.uk/news/northern-ireland/long-running-legal-aid-dispute-resolved/34445432.html.

[38] *Department of Finance, Land and Property Services v Foster* [2022] NICA 19.

[39] *A Health and Social Care Trust v A Mother* [2022] NICA 63.

[40] *Re Downey's Application* [2022] NICA 67.

4.4 Appeals from the High Court in judicial review cases

Of the 566 reported appeals from the High Court between 1999 and 2023, 300 (53 per cent) were in cases involving applications for judicial review.[41] A significant distinguishing feature of such applications is that they can proceed to a full hearing only if leave to bring the application has first been obtained. If leave is refused, there can either be an appeal against that refusal to the Court of Appeal or a fresh application can be made to the Court of Appeal: there is no significant difference in the two modes of proceeding.[42] The test that the Court of Appeal applies when deciding whether to grant leave is the same as that applied by the High Court; namely, that there must be an arguable case which either has a reasonable prospect of success[43] or is fit for further investigation by the Court.[44] When the Court of Appeal is considering whether to grant leave and does so, it often proceeds to deal with the merits of the appeal in what is called a 'rolled-up' hearing. Having granted leave it can also order that the case should proceed as if it had been commenced by a writ for a civil claim, because proceeding by way of judicial review is deemed inappropriate.[45]

---

[41] See, generally, Judicature (NI) Act 1978, ss 18–21 and RCJ (NI) 1980, Order 53.

[42] *Re OV's (A Minor) Application* [2021] NICA 58, citing the Privy Council's decision in *Kemper Reinsurance Co v Minister of Finance of Bermuda* [2000] 1 AC 1. There, Lord Hoffmann said that leave to apply for judicial review is different from leave to appeal, and so the rule in *Lane v Esdaile*, n 17, does not apply.

[43] *Re Burns' Application* [2022] NICA 20, [28], per Keegan LCJ, citing *Re Omagh District Council's Application* [2004] NICA 10.

[44] *Beatty v Director of Public Prosecutions* [2022] NICA 13, [39], per McCloskey LJ; *Re Ní Chuinneagain's Application* [2022] NICA 56, [34]-[44]. For more on this test, see Gordon Anthony, *Judicial Review in Northern Ireland* (3rd edn, Hart Publishing 2024) 70–1.

[45] *Leszkiewicz v Secretary of State for the Home Department* [2022] NICA 24: rather than proceed by way of judicial review the applicant should have sued for false imprisonment.

Judicial review applications are designated as civil cases even though they involve issues connected with the criminal justice system. Confusingly, however, judicial review applications which are specifically 'in a criminal cause or matter' are *not* within the jurisdiction of the Court of Appeal: they must first be dealt with by a Divisional Court of the Queen's Bench Division of the High Court, which will comprise at least two High Court judges or Lords/Ladies Justices.[46] The only avenue of appeal from the Divisional Court is directly to the UK Supreme Court.[47] Crucially, however, this avenue is available to 'the defendant or the prosecutor' in the Divisional Court case, but *not* to the applicant.[48]

The boundary line around what qualifies as 'a criminal cause or matter' is not always easy to discern. It was closely examined by the Supreme Court in a case from Northern Ireland in 2020, *Re McGuinness's Application*, where the issue was how to calculate the expiry date of a tariff imposed on a sentenced prisoner.[49] The Supreme Court ruled that it had no jurisdiction to deal with the case because it had come directly from the Divisional Court in Northern Ireland when it ought to have been heard by the Court of Appeal. It therefore remitted the case to the Court of Appeal.[50] Two years later two further cases relating to release dates were heard by that Court.[51] In

---

[46] RCJ (NI) 1980, Order 53, r 2.

[47] Judicature (NI) Act 1978, s 41(1)(a). See too s 35(2)(a). The position is similar in England and Wales: see the Administration of Justice Act 1960, s 1(1)(a).

[48] Ibid, s 41(6)(a) spells out what 'defendant' means in s 41.

[49] [2020] UKSC 6, [2021] AC 392.

[50] *Re McGuinness's Application (No 1)* [2020] NICA 54, where the Court of Appeal allowed the Department's appeal against the Divisional Court's decision.

[51] *Re Conway's Application* [2022] NICA 18. See too *Leszkiewicz v Secretary of State for the Home Department*, n 45, where the applicant complained that he was being kept in custody beyond his release date just because the Home Office had not yet completed the paperwork on his deportation.

that same year it heard an appeal against a High Court judge's refusal to grant leave for judicial review of the police's failure to provide information about the progress it was making with an investigation into the death of the appellant's brother: this was because there was not yet 'a criminal cause or matter' involved.[52]

The question needs to be asked whether it continues to be justifiable to treat judicial review applications in a criminal cause or matter differently from applications in any other cause or matter. Applicants in criminal causes benefit from having at least two judges consider their applications at first instance but they cannot appeal. Applicants in civil causes benefit from being able to appeal at two levels, subject to leave being granted for the second appeal to the Supreme Court. If cases are urgent they can be expedited, whether they are criminal or civil in nature. The leapfrog appeal procedure can also be used.[53]

The current situation exists even though a 1970 report by a committee chaired by Lord MacDermott, which preceded the Judicature (NI) Act 1978, recommended that Divisional Courts should be abolished and that the Court of Appeal should have jurisdiction to hear and determine appeals 'from any judgment or order of the High Court'.[54] Noting this, McCloskey J, as he then was, ventured to say in *Re JR 27's Application* that '[t]here may well be a case for reinstating this proposal now and, as regards this issue, there is unanimity of opinion amongst the members of this present chamber of

---

[52] *Frizzell v The Police Service of Northern Ireland* [2022] NICA 14. See too *Beatty v Director of Public Prosecutions*, n 44, seeking an order that the DPP had a discretionary power to direct the Chief Constable to accelerate the police investigation into the death of the applicant's brother.

[53] This is where an appeal can go straight from the High Court to the Supreme Court because, for example, there would be little point in the Court of Appeal considering the case as it too would be bound by a precedent which was binding on the High Court. See the Administration of Justice Act 1969, ss 12–16.

[54] *Report of the Committee on the Supreme Court of Judicature of Northern Ireland* (Cmnd 4292, 1970), para 231.

judges'.[55] He was supported on that point by both Morgan LCJ and Weatherup LJ in the same case.[56]

The Review of Civil Justice in Northern Ireland adopted the same stance in 2017:

> There is no reason to retain this distinction, which is complex and now anachronistic, and it should be abolished. This could be achieved by a relatively straightforward statutory amendment to the Judicature (Northern Ireland) Act 1978.[57] ... In this jurisdiction, there is no reason to believe that the provision of a right of appeal to the Court of Appeal in [criminal] cases would significantly increase the workload of the court. The requirement to appeal directly to the UKSC now seems anomalous and has been the subject of adverse judicial comment.[58]

The latest judicial affirmation of this position comes from Scoffield J,[59] who is also the current Chair of the Northern Ireland Law Commission, a body which is conducting further research in this field. We touch upon this issue again in Chapter 8, where the views of our judicial interviewees are summarised.

---

[55] [2010] NIQB 12, [16].

[56] Ibid, [50]–[51].

[57] Here the Review cites *Re Barry Morgan* [2015] NIQB 60, [9], per Morgan LCJ. See *Review Group's Report on Civil Justice*, n 2, para 20.20. The Review immediately adds, however, that in any judicial review case the rules of court should still permit a Divisional Court to be assembled where a judge considers it to be necessary.

[58] Ibid, *Review Group's Report on Civil Justice*, n 2, para 20.3. A footnote in this paragraph is inaccurate: it should actually refer to *Re JR 27's Application* [2010] NIQB 12.

[59] *Re Diver's and Corrigan's Applications* [2021] NIQB 84, [18]: 'I would add my voice to those before me who have expressed the view that the distinction is now anachronistic and serves no useful purpose – or at least no purpose outweighing the disadvantages of the distinction being maintained.'

It is also clear that in Northern Ireland there cannot be a judicial review of a ruling by the Crown Court, which tries serious criminal offences. This is because the Crown Court and the High Court are of equal standing. In England and Wales, however, legislation allows the High Court to entertain applications for judicial review of decisions by the Crown Court provided they relate to matters other than a trial on indictment.[60] Both the Divisional Court and the Court of Appeal in that jurisdiction have held, for example, that a Crown Court order removing reporting restrictions is not a matter relating to trial on indictment and so it can be judicially reviewed by the High Court.[61] When such a case came before the Court of Appeal in Northern Ireland it had to hold that it had no jurisdiction to process it.[62] The Court then proceeded, remarkably, to write words into existing legislation; namely, section 159(1)(c) of the Criminal Justice Act 1988, which applies in England and Wales too, so that it now reads:

> a person aggrieved may appeal to the Court of Appeal, if that court grants leave, against ... (c) any order restricting the publication of any report of the whole or any part of a trial on indictment or any such ancillary proceedings *or any discharge of such order or refusal by the Court to make such order*; and the decision of the Court of Appeal shall be final.[63]

4.5 Appeals by way of case stated or otherwise on a point of law

Besides the Magistrates' Courts (NI) Order 1981 and the County Courts (NI) Order 1980,[64] various other statutes allow

---

[60] Senior Courts Act 1981, s 29(3).

[61] *R v Leicester Crown Court, ex parte S (a Minor) (Note)* [1993] 1 WLR 111 (Div Ct); *R v Lee* [1993] 2 All ER 170 (CA).

[62] *R v McGreechan* [2014] NICA 5, [2015] NI 44.

[63] Ibid, [24], per Morgan LCJ. The italicised words are those written in by the Court.

[64] Procedures in such cases are governed by Order 59, r 61 of the RCJ (NI) 1980.

for appeals to the Court of Appeal by way of case stated or on points of law.[65] In the 25 years under review, as is evident from Table 4.1, there were 174 reported appeals in this category (24 per cent of all reported civil appeals), by far the largest sub-categories being appeals from industrial tribunals and the Fair Employment Tribunal (15 per cent of all reported civil appeals).

It is even possible for a High Court judge to state a case for the opinion of the Court of Appeal if the High Court has heard an appeal in a civil case from a county court.[66] This happened just twice during the period under review.[67] In *A Father v A Mother* the Court confirmed that it has no jurisdiction to hear an appeal against a High Court order in an appeal from a Family Care Centre (a version of a county court) *except* by way of case stated,[68] but in *Registrar of Companies v JP Murphy Ltd* it held that it had no jurisdiction at all to hear an appeal against the *refusal* of a High Court judge to state a case.[69]

In 2009 the case stated procedure in Northern Ireland attracted trenchant criticism from the House of Lords, just before it transitioned into the Supreme Court. This was in *SCA Packaging Ltd v Boyle*, where a company challenged the claim by an employee that she was disabled and the Court of Appeal, in holding that she was, applied a different test from that used in

---

[65] For example, the Lands Tribunal and Compensation Act (NI) 1964, s 8(6); Rates (NI) Order 1977, arts 30B(5)(c), 30C(11)(b), 30D(9)(b), and 31A(12C); Judgments Enforcement (NI) Order 1981, art 140(3); Social Security Administration (NI) Act 1992, s 22; Industrial Tribunals (NI) Order 1996, art 22; Fair Employment and Treatment (NI) Order 1998, art 90; Tribunals, Courts and Enforcement Act 2007, s 13(12) (concerning appeals from the Upper Tribunal).

[66] County Courts (NI) Order 1980, art 62. Any decision by the Court of Appeal in such a case is 'final', but see *Lee v Ashers Baking Co Ltd* [2018] UKSC 49, [2019] 1 All ER 1.

[67] *Cunningham v Police Service of Northern Ireland* [2016] NICA 58, [2019] NI 52; *DMcA v A Health and Social Services Trust* [2017] NICA 3, [2019] NI 219.

[68] [2022] NICA 52.

[69] [2021] NICA 62.

England and Wales.[70] The case took a long time to reach the
Court of Appeal, partly because of the case stated procedure.
Legislation allowed a party to industrial tribunal proceedings
to either appeal to the Court of Appeal or to require the
tribunal to state a case for the Court of Appeal's opinion –
but only in accordance with rules of court.[71] Unfortunately,
those rules provided solely for the latter option.[72] This meant
that, even though a tribunal had already provided a thorough
judgment on a dispute, it was then required to specify exactly
what questions should be sent to the Court of Appeal for its
opinion. In *Boyle* that process (admittedly partly due to the
chairperson's illness) took almost a year to complete. Lord
Hope called for the rules of court in Northern Ireland to be
reformed, as they had been in Scotland, so that the questions
for case stated are settled early on and a timetable is then set for
the draft case to be commented upon by the parties. He added
that: 'Properly used, the stated case procedure can provide a
very useful vehicle for bringing issues of law before the court.
But it must not be allowed to act as a brake on their prompt
determination, as has unfortunately happened in this case.'[73]
Lady Hale was equally critical of the procedure:

> It is suitable for appeals on points of law from courts or
> tribunals which do not routinely explain their decisions.
> But aside from the duplication of effort and delay, it can
> give rise to unseemly debates between the tribunal and
> the parties as to the issues upon which a case should be
> stated. It is the appeal court, rather than the tribunal

---

[70] [2009] UKHL 37, [2009] 4 All ER 1181. The CA decision is at [2008]
NI 48, [2009] NIJB 285.

[71] Industrial Tribunals (NI) Order 1996, art 22(1).

[72] RCJ (NI) 1980, Order 61, r 1.

[73] See n 70, [17]. At [82] Lord Neuberger agreed that in this case 'the [case
stated] procedure has proved itself to be worse than unsatisfactory' and
at [45] Lord Rodger associated himself with the remarks by both Lord
Hope and Lord Neuberger.

under appeal, which should decide which issues are worthy of its attention.[74]

Lord Brown added that the case stated procedure, as opposed to a straightforward appeal by leave, 'has nothing whatever to commend it – and much by way of needless delay, expense and general aggravation in its disfavour'. He called for this 'absurdity' to be eradicated.[75]

Less than three months after the House of Lords' remarks, the Court of Appeal in Northern Ireland endorsed them in *Rogan v South Eastern Health and Social Care Trust*.[76] Morgan LCJ directed that his judgment should be sent to the joint secretaries of the Court of Judicature Rules Committee so that work could begin as a matter of urgency to enable appeals from industrial tribunals to proceed by way of appeal on a point of law rather than by case stated.[77] A new rule of court was duly drafted and came into effect on 1 April 2010.[78]

The *Rogan* case also illustrates how the Court of Appeal serves as a supervisory body of tribunals and lower courts. Morgan LCJ quoted from an earlier judgment by Girvan LJ where he urged industrial tribunals to avoid becoming increasingly costly by better controlling the length of their proceedings.[79] They should do so by constantly bearing in mind the 'overriding objective' of the regulations governing industrial tribunals; namely, to enable tribunals to deal with cases justly, which means, so far as practicable, ensuring that parties are on an equal footing, that cases are dealt with in ways which are proportionate to the complexity or importance of

---

[74] Ibid, [75].

[75] Ibid, [79].

[76] [2009] NICA 47, per Morgan LCJ and Girvan LJ.

[77] Ibid, [30].

[78] Order 60B, added by the Rules of the Court of Judicature (NI) (Amendment) 2010.

[79] Ibid, [20], citing *Peifer v Castlederg High School and Western Education and Library Board* [2008] NICA 49, [2]–[4].

the issues, that the proceedings are expeditious and fair, and that expense is saved.

4.6 Conclusion

This chapter has sought to explain and critique the civil jurisdiction of the Court of Appeal. It confirms that that jurisdiction is wide-ranging and that there are several aspects of it which are ripe for reform. A recommendation of the Civil Justice Review that responsibility for overall management of the Court's civil work should be allocated to a particular Lord or Lady Justice has so far not been implemented. A Shadow Civil Justice Council has been established, meeting at least twice a year, but it has not yet considered any issue specifically related to the Court of Appeal.[80] We hope that this chapter will be a stimulus for further debate and reform.

---

[80] See www.judiciaryni.uk/shadow-civil-justice-council, where the minutes of the Council's meetings can be found.

FIVE

Criminal Business

5.1 Introduction

This chapter opens with an overview of the types of criminal appeals and references which the Court of Appeal has dealt with during the past 25 years. It then looks at each type of appeal or reference in more detail, focusing on the tests that are applied by the Court when deciding frequently recurring questions. The chapter highlights that while some research suggests the Court of Appeal did not do all that it might have done to ensure fair trials during some years of the troubles, there is no evidence to suggest that it suffers from failings of the same kind today.

5.2 Types of criminal appeals and references

Between 1999 and 2023 there were 1,961 criminal disposals in the Court of Appeal, which accounted for 49 per cent of all disposals. As regards the reported cases during that period, 723 were criminal cases, again representing 49 per cent of all reported cases. Table 5.1 indicates the number and percentage of each type of reported appeal and reference.

This is a substantial workload in a specialised area of law, especially given that some judges appointed to the Court of Appeal may have had little experience of criminal work in their careers up to that point. We know that significant training opportunities are available to judges who try

Table 5.1: Number and percentage of reported criminal appeals and references, 1999–2023

Type of appeal or reference	Number of reported cases	Percentage of all reported criminal cases
Appeals from the Crown Court against conviction or against conviction and sentence	300	42%
Appeals from the Crown Court against sentence only	214	30%
References from the Director of Public Prosecutions or Attorney General	83	11%
Appeals from magistrates' or county courts by way of case stated	75	10%
References from the Criminal Cases Review Commission	22	3%
Prosecution appeals from rulings by Crown Court judges	15	2%
Other cases*	14	2%
Total	723	100%

* These include, for example, cases on whether there should be a retrial, whether leave should be granted to appeal to the House of Lords, and whether solicitor advocates can represent appellants in criminal appeals.

criminal cases in Northern Ireland, at whatever level, but we are not aware of any training that focuses on criminal appellate work (apart from 'on the job' training when High Court judges are asked to sit in Court of Appeal cases). However, at least one of the judges sitting in a criminal case in the Court of Appeal is certain to have substantial expertise in criminal appellate work. If necessary, a retired judge with such expertise can be called upon to supplement that of the other judges. We know, too, that legal researchers provide more assistance with criminal appeals than they do with civil appeals.[1]

We have already noted that dissenting judgments are very rare across the board within Court of Appeal decisions, and in criminal appeals they are like hen's teeth. Under English law, the Court of Appeal must give only a single judgment unless the presiding judge thinks it is convenient for more than one opinion to be given.[2] This is not a legal requirement in Northern Ireland, but it is certainly the common practice. In the 25 years under review, there were dissents in only two criminal cases. One was by Weir LJ in *Director of Public Prosecutions v Douglas*, where he disagreed that a District Judge was legally correct in amending a complaint of taking and driving away to one of vehicle interference.[3] The other, more significant, was by Treacy LJ in *R v Wilson*, which was an appeal brought in 2022 against a conviction in 1978 for explosive offences by a woman who wanted to adduce medical evidence in her defence.[4] Treacy LJ would have held in her favour, but he was out-voted by two retired judges, Sir Declan Morgan and Sir Paul Maguire.

In the course of their judgments judges in criminal appeals have at times made suggestions as to how aspects of the criminal justice system should be improved. In *R v Foronda* they specified how exactly interpreters should be appointed;[5] in *R v McCauley* they strongly criticised the police and security services for mishandling important evidence;[6] and in *R v Doherty* they

---

[1]   In *Police Service of NI v O'Donnell* [2008] NICA 9, at [18], the Court admitted that research had been carried out for it by a legal officer of the Court. See too Chapter 3.

[2]   Senior Courts Act 1981, s 59. For an excellent analysis, see Rory Kelly, 'Criminalising Dissent' (2022) 138 *LQR* 432.

[3]   [2016] NICA 14.

[4]   [2022] NICA 73 and 74.

[5]   [2014] NICA 17.

[6]   [2014] NICA 60.

condemned the failure of Northern Ireland's post-sentencing system to rehabilitate offenders.[7]

5.3 Appeals against rulings in the Crown Court

As a criminal trial proceeds through the Crown Court the judge sometimes has to make decisions on subsidiary issues. In 2004 legislation was passed making it clear that the prosecution as well as the defendant can appeal against such decisions, subject to certain conditions, one of which is that the prosecution must agree that if leave to appeal is not obtained or if the appeal is abandoned then the defendant should be acquitted in relation to the offence in question.[8] The first such appeal occurred in *R v Grindy*, where the Court refused leave because, contrary to rules of court, the application had not been made immediately after the judge's ruling had been given.[9] The Court of Appeal has since made it clear that it takes a strict stance on the need for all the conditions to be satisfied before it will even consider any such appeal.[10] To date there have been 15 reported cases dealing with prosecution appeals under the 2004 Order.

5.4 Appeals against convictions in the Crown Court

Most appeals against convictions (and sentences) in the Crown Court require leave to appeal.[11] The exception is appeals

---

[7]   [2022] NICA 4, [53]–[57].

[8]   Criminal Justice (NI) Order 2004, Pt IV (arts 16–33), especially art 17(8) and (9).

[9]   [2006] NICA 10, [2006] NI 290; see too the Crown Court (Prosecution Appeals) Rules (NI) 2005, r 2(1).

[10]   *R v JM* [2013] NICA 64, [2015] NI 8, where the prosecution sought to appeal against a judge's ruling that the proceedings should be stayed because of an abuse of process.

[11]   For more details see John Stannard, *Northern Ireland Criminal Procedure: An Introduction* (Round Hall Sweet & Maxwell 2000) 181–6.

against judgments issued by a judge sitting alone, without a jury, in cases involving offences connected to proscribed organisations. These judge–only courts were first introduced in Northern Ireland in 1973,[12] following a review chaired by Lord Diplock.[13] They catered for terrorist-related cases where there could be a risk of jurors being biased or intimidated. Such trials can still be heard today under a provision which has been renewed every two years since it was introduced in 2007.[14] Defendants in such cases are entitled to receive a written judgment from the judge setting out the reasons for their decision[15] and as a quid pro quo for the absence of a jury defendants have an automatic right of appeal.[16] Judge-only trials are also permitted in non-terrorist cases (as in England and Wales) if there is a danger of jury tampering, as occurred in *R v Mackle*[17] and *R v McStravick*,[18] but in such cases leave is still required for an appeal. Genevieve Lennon and Clive Walker have recently argued that if juryless trials are to continue in Northern Ireland it should be under this scheme alone.[19]

When leave to appeal is required the party appealing can have two bites of the cherry. They can first apply to a 'single judge' and if they fail at that stage they can re-apply to a full Court of Appeal, usually comprising three judges.[20] As with

---

[12] Northern Ireland (Emergency Provisions) Act 1973, s 2.

[13] *Report of the Commission to consider legal procedures to deal with terrorist activities in Northern Ireland* (Cmnd 5185, 1972).

[14] Justice and Security (NI) Act 2007, ss 1–9; Justice and Security (NI) Act 2007 (Extension of Duration of Non-jury Trial Provisions) Order 2023.

[15] In *R v McCourt* [2010] NICA 6 the Court of Appeal overturned a conviction from 1977 on the ground that the judge in question, McGonigal LJ, had not issued a reasoned judgment.

[16] n 14, s 5(6) and (7).

[17] [2007] NICA 37, [2008] NI 183.

[18] [2010] NICA 34.

[19] 'Half a century of non-jury trials in Northern Ireland, Part 1: Origins and Frameworks' [2024] *Crim LR* 142; 'Part 2: Future Options' [2024] *Crim LR* 208.

[20] Criminal Appeal (NI) Act 1980, s 44(1)–(2).

civil cases, the Court will often grant leave and then proceed immediately to decide whether to allow the appeal on its merits in a 'rolled-up' hearing. Single judges have other powers too; for example, to extend the time for giving notice of appeal, to grant leave for an appellant to be present at any proceedings, to allow the appellant to appear by a live link, or to order a witness to attend for examination.[21]

The time limit for making applications for leave to appeal is 28 days after the conviction (or sentence) has been announced, but this period 'may be extended at any time by the Court'.[22] As can be imagined, there are a high number of applications for leave to appeal out of time and in the criminal sphere the precedent which now applies in such scenarios is *R v Brownlee*.[23] Morgan LCJ set out six principles, too detailed to repeat in full here, but the most important is that an extension of time will usually be granted, even after a considerable delay, 'if there appears to be merit in the grounds of appeal'.[24] This inevitably means that the Court has to go into the merits of an appeal in some detail before it is able to decide whether the appeal should be allowed to proceed.

Regarding the Court's approach to whether to allow a criminal appeal, it now frequently refers to the basic principles laid down by Kerr LCJ, as he then was, in *R v Pollock*:

(1) The Court of Appeal should concentrate on the single and simple question 'does it think that the verdict is unsafe'.

---

[21] Ibid, s 45.

[22] Ibid, s 16(1)–(2). In civil cases the usual time limit for appeals is six weeks: see Chapter 4.

[23] [2015] NICA 39.

[24] Ibid, [8(ii)] and [8(vi)]. In *R v McLaughlin* [2022] NICA 64, a sub-postmaster who was wrongly convicted of false accounting succeeded in his appeal 17 years later.

(2) This exercise does not involve trying the case again. Rather it requires the Court, where conviction has followed trial and no fresh evidence has been introduced on the appeal, to examine the evidence given at trial and to gauge the safety of the verdict against that background.

(3) The Court should eschew speculation as to what may have influenced the jury to its verdict.

(4) The Court of Appeal must be persuaded that the verdict is unsafe but if, having considered the evidence, the Court has a significant sense of unease about the correctness of the verdict based on a reasoned analysis of the evidence, it should allow the appeal.[25]

A common ground for allowing an appeal is that the trial judge did not give a proper direction to the jury. Among the errors which have led to a successful appeal are inviting a jury to draw inferences from a defendant's silence,[26] not explaining to the jury why it should not return a verdict of manslaughter rather than murder,[27] and not dealing fully with the defence of duress.[28] At times the Court has identified four or five aspects in which the trial judge has failed to properly direct the jury,[29] but it has also pointed out that a direction was far too long.[30] On that last occasion it cited Lord Hailsham's words in *R v Lawrence*:

[25] [2004] NICA 34, [32], commenting on the Criminal Appeal (NI) Act 1980, s 2, which reads: 'Subject to the provisions of this Act, the Court of Appeal (a) shall allow an appeal against conviction if it thinks that the conviction is unsafe; and (b) shall dismiss such an appeal in any other case.'

[26] *R v Haughey* [2001] NICA 12.

[27] *R v King* [2005] NICA 20.

[28] *Forrester v Leckey* [2005] NICA 26 and *R v Hutchinson* [2006] NICA 47.

[29] See, for example, *R v AG* [2010] NICA 20; *R v McCalmont* [2010] NICA 27.

[30] *R v Meehan* [2011] NICA 10, [2012] NIJB 91.

The purpose of a direction to a jury is not best achieved by a disquisition on jurisprudence or philosophy or a universally applicable circular tour round the area of law affected by the case. The search for universally applicable definitions is often productive of more obscurity than light. A direction is seldom improved and may be considerably damaged by copious recitations from the total content of a judge's note book.[31]

The Court of Appeal has itself been known to get things wrong. In one case it allowed an application for leave to appeal to be re-opened so that it could consider whether its mistake ought to have led it to allow the appeal.[32] As we shall see later, several of the Court's decisions during the troubles have subsequently been overturned following references from the Criminal Cases Review Commission. On the other hand, in the 1980s the Court of Appeal itself overturned many convictions resulting from trials in which multiple defendants were prosecuted simultaneously relying on information supplied by 'supergrasses'.[33] Steven Greer meticulously charted the collapse of the supergrass phenomenon and concluded that:

The Northern Ireland Court of Appeal simply accepted that the trial judge in each case had been too willing to believe the supergrass evidence and had paid insufficient attention to the specific weaknesses which had been exposed by the defence. No new evidence and no novel arguments were necessary to achieve this result, and indeed most of the judges who sat in each of the appeal hearings had themselves convicted on the uncorroborated evidence

---

[31] [1982] AC 510, 519.

[32] *R v Maughan* [2004] NICA 21. The Court still dismissed the appeal.

[33] Steven Greer calculates that in the five Court of Appeal supergrass cases 66 of the 78 convictions were quashed: *Supergrasses: A Study in Anti-Terrorist Law Enforcement in Northern Ireland* (Clarendon Press 1995) 287.

of other supergrasses. ... [T]hese decisions appear to have been the result of a deliberate change in judicial policy.[34]

A further frequent ground of appeal is abuse of process, which can take the form, for instance, of excessive delay, breaches of the rules on disclosure or some other unfairness. In this context Girvan LJ has said:

> The function of the Court of Appeal, accordingly, is to consider the overall safety of the convictions. Since the court must review the whole case to consider the safety of the conviction it is, accordingly, bound to consider the entirety of the trial process and not simply whether at a point in the trial the judge could or should have stayed the proceedings.[35]

The position of the Court regarding its power to admit fresh evidence in an appeal was explained by McCloskey LJ in *R v Ferris*, where he referred to section 25 of the Criminal Appeal (NI) Act 1980:

> [The power] is expressly fettered only by what the court considers necessary or expedient in the interests

---

[34] Ibid, 173–4. Lowry LCJ presided in four of the five Court of Appeal supergrass cases: *R v Graham* [1984] 18 NIJB 1 (where O'Donnell LJ made it clear, countering Hutton J, that he entertained 'considerable doubt as to whether the fact that a witness may be shown by independent evidence to be probably telling the truth as against one defendant, can be used to support his credibility against all the other accused'); *R v Donnelly* [1986] 4 NIJB 32; *R v Crumley* [1986] 14 NIJB 30; and *R v Steenson* [1986] 17 NIJB 36. In the fifth case Lowry LCJ was himself the trial judge; most of his judgment was overturned, with a rare dissent: *R v Gibney* [1986] 4 NIJB 4 (O'Donnell LJ would have allowed Gibney's own appeal). For a further concise account of the supergrass phenomenon see John Jackson and Sean Doran, *Judge Without Jury: Diplock Trials in the Adversary System* (Clarendon Press 1995) 44–7.

[35] *R v Fulton* [2009] NICA 39, [54].

of justice. Notably, the factors listed in section 25(2) do not constitute an exhaustive checklist. Thus the court is at liberty to weigh other factors which it considers relevant. No procedural formalities are prescribed. The court is empowered to admit new evidence either upon application or acting of its motion.[36]

Notwithstanding the apparent breadth of this discretionary power, it is not usually exercised in favour of the appellant. In *R v DPMC*,[37] for example, the Court refused to admit new evidence from a Professor of Psychology on 'autobiographical memory': it shared concerns already expressed by the Court of Appeal in England and Wales about the research in question.[38]

When the Court of Appeal allows an appeal and is considering whether the defendant should be retried, the test it applies is again whether a retrial would be in the interests of justice having regard to all the circumstances of the case. This is laid down by statute[39] and has not been expanded upon to any great extent by appeal judges in Northern Ireland, or by those in England and Wales.[40] In *R v Hewitt and Anderson*, Nicholson LJ said:

> The decision whether to order a re-trial requires an exercise of judgment involving the public interest and

---

[36] [2020] NICA 60, [2021] NIJB 627, [21]. The judge cited in support, among other cases, *R v Walsh* [2007] NI 154 and *R v McDonald (AG's References 11 to 13 of 2005)* [2006] NICA 4, [2006] NIJB 424.

[37] [2010] NICA 22. See too *R v Jamison* [2023] NICA 51, where the accused belatedly sought to adduce evidence that he was a state agent.

[38] See, for example, *R v Bowman* [2006] EWCA Crim 417.

[39] Criminal Appeal (NI) Act 1980, s 6(1).

[40] The relevant legislation in England and Wales is the Criminal Appeal Act 1968, s 7(1); in *R v Maxwell* [2010] UKSC 48, [2001] 1 WLR 1837 the Supreme Court upheld the decision to order a retrial even though the defendant's post-conviction admissions would not have been made had there not been gross police misconduct.

the legitimate interests of the appellants. One could set out a list of the various factors which have to be taken into account. But each decision turns on the facts of the individual case and there is little to be gained by comparing one case with another or in using a decision made in one case when deciding another case.[41]

A few of the cases reported during our 25-year period were devoted solely to the issue of whether a defendant should be re-tried following a successful appeal against conviction.[42]

If an appeal is unsuccessful the Court of Appeal retains a power to re-open it, although most allegations of a miscarriage of justice are likely to come to it by way of a reference from the Criminal Cases Review Commission established by the Criminal Appeal Act 1995.[43] In the case of *R v Walsh* a determined applicant who had for years declared his innocence of having been in possession of a coffee-jar bomb eventually succeeded in getting his appeal re-opened and his conviction quashed. In the course of that litigation Kerr LCJ said:

> We have concluded that the power of the Court of Appeal to re-list a case has not been removed by the 1995 Act. The occasion for the exercise of such a power will arise only in the most exceptional circumstances, however. ... Where CCRC has been invited to refer a conviction to the Court of Appeal for a second time and has declined, if this court considers that because the rules or well-established practice have not been followed or the earlier court was misinformed about some relevant matter and, in consequence, if the appeal is not re-listed, an injustice

---

[41] [2005] NICA 38, [6].

[42] For example, *R v CK* [2008] NICA 31, [2009] NIJB 149; *R v Daly* [2011] NICA 69; *R v TJ* [2018] NICA 31.

[43] See Section 5.7.

is likely to occur, it may have recourse to its inherent power to re-list (or, effectively, re-open) the appeal.[44]

5.5 Appeals against sentences in the Crown Court

As regards appeals against sentence,[45] the Court of Appeal's central tenet is that a sentence will be reduced only if it is deemed to be manifestly excessive or wrong in principle.[46] Unlike in England and Wales, however, the Court of Appeal in Northern Ireland can increase as well as decrease a sentence's severity, although it cannot increase a sentence 'by reason or in consideration of any evidence that was not given at the Crown Court'.[47] Recently, in *R v Maughan*,[48] the Court of Appeal suggested that the reason why discounts for a guilty plea tend to be lower in Northern Ireland than in England and Wales (maybe 25 per cent rather than 33 per cent) is that legal advice in England and Wales police stations may sometimes be given by advisors who are not fully qualified solicitors, which would not happen in Northern Ireland.[49]

R v McCandless is the leading authority in Northern Ireland on the principles that should be applied when establishing the

---

[44] [2007] NICA 4, [2007] NI 154, [31], and [2010] NICA 7 (where the Court allowed fresh fingerprint evidence to be admitted and quashed the conviction).

[45] See too Stannard, n 11, 186–8.

[46] *R v Newell* [1975] 4 NIJB 2. For a good example of a detailed approach to a sentencing appeal see *R v Nelson* [2020] NICA 7, where (at [20]) McCloskey LJ set out no fewer than 16 principles which he and his fellow judges took into consideration.

[47] Criminal Appeal (NI) Act 1980, s 10(3). See, for example, *R v Wooton* [2014] NICA 69, [2016] NIJB 210.

[48] [2019] NICA 66, [76]-[82]. The Supreme Court dismissed a further appeal in this case ([2022] UKSC 13, [2022] 1 WLR 2820), the judgment being given by Sir Declan Morgan, the retired LCJ of Northern Ireland.

[49] In *R v Anderson* [2021] NICA 28, [2022] NI 135, Morgan LCJ set out what steps should be taken if counsel have discussions with a judge about

categories of sentence for murder.[50] The Court emulated the practice already adopted in England and Wales,[51] although it emphasised that the Practice Statement in question was for guidance only. In a later Court of Appeal decision Morgan LCJ endorsed this position by saying that the factors mentioned in the Practice Statement 'are not, of course, intended to be comprehensive. They are intended to assist sentencers in assessing the culpability of the offender and the degree of harm caused by the offence. They are not to be applied mechanically or to be interpreted strictly as if they were a statute.'[52]

This reflects the general position in Northern Ireland, where there is no Sentencing Council such as there is in England and Wales.[53] Instead, there is a Lord/Lady Chief Justice's Sentencing Group, established in 2010.[54] This advises on sentencing guidelines for magistrates' courts and considers first instance judgments of the Crown Court and judgments of the Court of Appeal so as to be able to advise the Judicial Studies Board as to their suitability for inclusion on its Sentencing Guidelines and Guidance website.[55] The Guidelines of the Sentencing Council for England and Wales, including for cases dealt with by the Crown Court and Court of Appeal, are much more detailed as regards, for example, the maximum permissible sentence, the starting point and sentencing range for each specific offence, and examples of possible aggravating

---

possible sentences before pleas, citing *Attorney General's Reference (Nos 6 to 10 of 2005) (Rooney and others)* [2005] NICA 44, [2006] NICA 218.

[50] [2004] NICA 1.

[51] As set out in the Practice Statement issued by Lord Woolf CJ, reported at [2002] 3 All ER 413.

[52] *R v Brown* [2011] NICA 70, [2013] NIJB 210, [8].

[53] See www.sentencingcouncil.org.uk.

[54] See www.judiciaryni.uk/lady-chief-justices-sentencing-group. There is an expectation that the Chief Justice should take a strong role in sentencing appeals, for reasons set out in Chapter 8.

[55] See www.judiciaryni.uk/sentencing-guidelines-magistrates-court and www.judiciaryni.uk/sentencing-guidelines-northern-ireland.

or mitigating circumstances. The Guidelines in Northern Ireland are currently displayed as sets covering 19 different types of crimes, such as drug offences, road traffic offences, sexual offences, and terrorist offences. Each set contains links to relevant judgments but with no navigational aids for the reader. There are also 23 sets of guidelines on General Sentencing Issues, addressing topics such as dangerous offenders, guilty pleas, and mitigating circumstances. The relevant website also refers to 'Sentencing Guideline Papers' from other sources, including individual judges.[56] These deal with four complex sentencing areas: domestic violence and abuse; hate crime; manslaughter, attempted murder, and wounding with intent; and honour-based crime.

5.6 References from the Director of Public Prosecutions

The DPP for Northern Ireland can make two kinds of reference to the Court of Appeal in criminal cases. Until 2002 these powers lay with the Attorney General for Northern Ireland.[57]

The first kind of reference is where, after an acquittal, the DPP may ask for the opinion of the Court on a point of law which has arisen in the case, but the reference 'shall not affect the trial in relation to which the reference is made or any acquittal in that trial'.[58] In the 25-year period under review there appears to be only one reported case involving this kind of reference. This was *R v Z*, where Girvan J ruled that the 'Real' IRA was not a proscribed organisation for the purposes of the Terrorism Act 2000 and he duly acquitted a number of defendants who had been charged with belonging to a proscribed organisation. The point of law was referred to the Court of Appeal, which ruled that in law the 'Real' IRA *was*

---

[56] See www.judiciaryni.uk/sentencing-guidelines-northern-ireland.

[57] Justice (NI) Act 2002, s 41(5) and (6).

[58] Criminal Appeal (NI) Act 1980, s 15(4).

a proscribed organisation.[59] Even though this did not affect his acquittal, Z appealed the matter to the House of Lords, but unsuccessfully.[60]

There is a notorious example of this kind of reference made to the Court of Appeal earlier in its history (in its guise as the Court of Criminal Appeal).[61] In *Attorney General for Northern Ireland's Reference (No 1 of 1975)* a soldier on patrol had been acquitted of murder by a judge sitting without a jury. While searching for terrorists the soldier had shot dead an unarmed man, who had run away when challenged, in the honest and reasonable, but mistaken, belief that he was a terrorist. The Court was asked whether in such circumstances the soldier could be guilty of any crime and, if so, whether it would be murder or manslaughter. The Court's opinion was that if the soldier did commit a crime (which is a matter for the tribunal of fact) then the crime would be murder. The Crown then persuaded the Court to allow the matter to be appealed to the House of Lords,[62] where (with one dissent) they ruled that if the tribunal of fact finds that 'in the agony of the moment the accused may have acted intuitively or instinctively without foreseeing the likely consequences of his act beyond preventing the deceased from getting away' then he has committed no crime at all.[63] This is a much-criticised decision,[64] but it reflects badly on the House of Lords rather than on the Court of Appeal.

The second type of reference the DPP can make is under section 36 of the Criminal Justice Act 1988, which allows

---

[59] [2004] NICA 23, [2005] NI 106.

[60] [2005] UKHL, [2005] 2 AC 645.

[61] This was under the Criminal Appeal (NI) Act 1968, s 48A, inserted by the Criminal Justice Act 1972, s 63(3).

[62] [1977] AC 105.

[63] Ibid, 139, per Lord Diplock. Viscount Dilhorne dissented.

[64] See, for example, Jonathan Rogers, 'Justifying the Use of Firearms by Policemen and Soldiers: A Response to the Home Office's Review of the Law on the Use of Lethal Force' (1998) 18 *Legal Studies* 486.

the DPP to refer to the Court of Appeal a sentence imposed by the Crown Court if it relates to an offence triable only on indictment (or to certain other offences specified in secondary legislation) and the DPP thinks it is 'unduly lenient'.[65] Between 1999 and 2023 the Court of Appeal issued 82 reported decisions on such references. In the majority of cases it agreed that the sentence in question was unduly lenient and exercised its discretion to increase it. In a few references it found the sentence to be unduly lenient but declined to increase it because there were 'exceptional circumstances', such as that the convicted person had already served a significant proportion of their original sentence and it would subject them to 'double jeopardy' to impose a new sentence at the appeal stage.[66] In the remaining references the Court found the original sentence to be lenient, but not unduly so. It has recently stressed that the threshold which the DPP must cross in order to have a sentence increased is 'high and exacting'.[67]

5.7 References from the Criminal Cases Review Commission

Under sections 10 and 13 of the Criminal Appeal Act 1995, the Criminal Cases Review Commission (CCRC) can refer any conviction on indictment, or any sentence in such a case, to the Court of Appeal in Northern Ireland if it believes there is 'a real possibility' that the conviction or sentence would not be upheld. In the period under review the Court of Appeal considered 22 such references, 19 of which related to

---

[65] This power was transferred to the DPP from the Attorney General by the Justice (NI) Act 2002, s 41(5), but it did not become operational until 'justice' was devolved to Northern Ireland in 2010.

[66] For example, *DPP's Reference (No 5 of 2019)* [2020] NICA 1, [2021] NI 196; *R v Corr* [2019] NICA 64.

[67] *R v Ali* [2023] NICA 20, [2023] NI 415, [4]; *R v McKenna and Sheridan* [2023] NICA 43, [9].

convictions in troubles-related cases, the commonest reason for the reversal of a conviction being the prosecution's failure to disclose evidence at the trial which might have cast doubt on the defendant's guilt.[68] In non-troubles related cases the reason was the trial judge's alleged failure to give a proper direction to the jury.[69]

When looking back at 'historic' convictions the Court of Appeal follows the approach set out by Lord Bingham in the English case of *R v King*:

> In looking at the safety of the conviction it is relevant to consider whether and to what extent a suspect may have been denied rights which he should have enjoyed under the rules in force at the time and whether and to what extent he may have lacked protections which it was later thought right that he should enjoy.[70]

This statement was first approved by the Court of Appeal in Northern Ireland in *R v Gordon*,[71] and then again in *R v Mulholland*[72] and in *R v Brown*,[73] the last of these being the authority most frequently cited today. There is of course some ambiguity in Lord Bingham's test in that judicial opinions can reasonably differ over when it would be 'right' to apply latter-day protections retroactively. In a study published in 2014 Marny Requa concluded – based on an examination of 38 cases referred by the CCRC between 1997 and 2013 – that: 'The

---

[68] See, for example, *R v Livingstone* [2013] NICA 33; *R v McCauley* [2014] NICA 60, [2016] NIJB 151; *R v Newell* [2014] NICA 87; *R v Ryan* [2014] NICA 72; *R v Devine* [2021] NICA 7.
[69] *R v Chakwane* [2013] NICA 24; *R v RH* [2018] NICA 28.
[70] [2000] 2 Cr App R 391, 402.
[71] [2001] NIJB 50.
[72] [2006] NICA 32, [2007] NIJB 152.
[73] [2012] NICA 14, [2013] NI 116. Cited with approval in *R v Livingstone*, n 68.

referred cases, although a small census, confirm that during the conflict [in Northern Ireland], the judiciary failed to recognize and respond to abuses of power and credible evidence of human rights violations perpetrated by security forces. The cases also demonstrate a persistently deferential approach in counterterrorism jurisprudence.'[74]

In a subsequent piece Requa suggested that the ruling in *R v Brown* effectively precludes the CCRC from making references to the Court of Appeal if the main faults in the earlier trial relate to detention or interrogation regimes, rather than, say, failures in disclosure.[75] Her prediction has largely been borne out to date, although a reference *was* made in *R v Goodall*, where the appellant argued that notes taken by the police during his interrogations had been doctored. The Court, however, was content that on the facts the police's notes were reliable and so the appeal was dismissed.[76] There was another unsuccessful reference from the CCRC in *R v O'Hagan*, where a conviction for causing an explosion in Derry in 1973 was upheld even though the Public Prosecution Service offered no opposition to the appeal. The Court simply had no sense of unease about the reliability of the defendant's admissions at the time.[77] In *R v Skinner*, rather than grant leave out of time to six appellants who alleged they had been wrongly convicted of murder or manslaughter under the doctrine of joint enterprise, which had later been liberalised by the UK Supreme Court's decision in

---

[74] Marny Requa, 'Considering Just-World Thinking in Counterterrorism Cases: Miscarriages of Justice in Northern Ireland' (2014) *Harvard Human Rights Journal* 7, 45.

[75] Marny Requa, 'Revisiting the Past: Miscarriages of Justice, the Courts and Transition' in Anne-Marie McAlinden and Clare Dwyer (eds), *Criminal Justice in Transition: The Northern Ireland Context* (Hart Publishing 2015) 251, 263–4. See too Hannah Quirk, 'Don't Mention the War: the Court of Appeal, the Criminal Cases Review Commission and Dealing with the Past in Northern Ireland' (2013) 76 *MLR* 949.

[76] [2018] NICA 24.

[77] [2015] NICA 63.

R v Jogee,[78] the Court of Appeal suggested that the appellants should think of asking the CCRC to refer their cases to the Court.[79]

5.8 Appeals by way of case stated

The statutory gateways for appeals to the Court of Appeal in criminal cases by way of case stated (where a question of law is put to the Court for its opinion) are article 146 of the Magistrates' Courts (NI) Order 1981 and article 61 of the County Courts (NI) Order 1980. The Court of Appeal cannot hear criminal appeals from either of these inferior courts in any other way than through the case stated procedure.[80]

The 1981 Order provides that an application for a case to be stated has to be made within 14 days of the day that the decision of the magistrates' court was given and the court must then state a case within a further three months.[81] There is no statutory provision allowing the Court of Appeal to extend either of these time limits, but whether they are mandatory or directive will, according to *Dillon v Chief Constable of the Police Service of Northern Ireland*,[82] albeit that was a decision on cases stated by a county court, depend on the particular facts of the case. When dealing with a case stated the Court of Appeal can exercise all the jurisdiction of the magistrates' court and it may affirm, reverse, or vary the decision of that court, remit the case to the magistrates' court with such declarations or directions as the Court of Appeal thinks proper, and make orders on costs and expenses as it thinks proper.[83] Between

---

78 [2016] UKSC 8, [2017] AC 387.

79 [2016] NICA 40, [2019] NI 1.

80 See too Stannard, n 11, 179–81.

81 Magistrates' Courts (NI) Order 1981, art 146(2) and (6).

82 [2016] NICA 15, [2018] NI 31.

83 Magistrates' Court (NI) Order 1981, art 147(1).

1999 and 2023 there were 65 reported criminal cases stated by magistrates' courts to the Court of Appeal.

If a court or tribunal refuses to state a case a litigant can apply to the Court of Appeal for an order requiring one to be stated. This occurred in two reported criminal appeals during the period under review: one failed[84] and one succeeded.[85] In the latter instance Deeny LJ took the opportunity to outline the procedures attached to stating a case. For a start, a magistrate can refuse an application to state a case only if it is 'frivolous',[86] although subsequent English case law suggests that here that word means 'futile, misconceived, hopeless or academic'.[87] Next, the magistrate should send a draft of any application for a case to be stated to the other parties in the case so that they can comment on it, leaving it to the magistrate to recast the document before it is 'crystallised' for the benefit of the Court of Appeal.[88] The Court of Appeal itself can later rephrase the questions submitted if it so desires.[89]

Procedures for cases stated under the County Courts (NI) Order 1980 differ from those applying to magistrates' courts in two respects. First, the applicant has 21 days, not 14, in which to make the application.[90] Second, while there is a statutory duty on a county court judge to state a case if an application is made, the judge can refuse to do so not only if they are of the opinion that the application is frivolous but also if it is 'vexatious or unreasonable'.[91] Between 1999 and 2023 there

---

[84] *Parker v Chief Constable of the Police Service of Northern Ireland* [2018] NICA 17.

[85] *Public Prosecution Service v Pearson* [2019] NICA 30.

[86] Magistrates' Courts (NI) Order 1981, art 146(4).

[87] *R v Mildenhall Magistrates' Court, ex parte Forest Heath District Council* [1997] EWCA Civ 1575 (30 April 1975).

[88] Magistrates' Courts Rules (NI) 1984, r 160(2) and (3).

[89] *Pearson*, n 85, [18].

[90] County Courts (NI) Order 1980, art 61(2).

[91] Ibid, art 61(1) and (4).

were ten reported criminal cases stated by county court judges to the Court of Appeal.

5.9 Conclusion

This chapter has analysed the various ways in which issues of criminal and sentencing law can reach the Court of Appeal. It has acknowledged that while there is research arguing the Court was too deferential to the security forces involved in criminal cases during the troubles, the modern-day Court is careful to adhere to the high standards of justice that a post-conflict society is entitled to expect. Today's judges adhere consistently to strict tests but always with an eye on fairness and the interests of justice. They almost always speak with one voice, thereby ensuring that the criminal law remains certain and comprehensible.

SIX

Conspicuous Business

6.1 Introduction

Court of Appeal judgments often precipitate a welter of journalistic and academic commentary. In this chapter we provide a thematic overview of the most conspicuous cases that have been handed down over the past 25 years based on our reading of the full case database and our analysis of secondary sources in which they have been discussed, such as academic journals and reputable media outlets. The chapter is divided into two parts. The first part explores politically sensitive cases and the second part examines human rights cases. These classifications overlap to some extent, but we trust they provide a helpful framework for navigating and remembering the long list of conspicuous cases that we have identified.

6.2 Politically sensitive cases

We have classified the cases in this section into two groups: constitutional disputes and conflict-related disputes.

6.2.1 Constitutional disputes

The Court of Appeal has been confronted by a broad range of constitutional cases. We will first highlight some of the most conspicuous public law challenges that the Court has decided when called upon to interpret the Belfast (Good Friday) Agreement and its statutory manifestations, before turning to some of the most conspicuous challenges that the Court has been required to determine as a consequence of Brexit.

6.2.1.1 The Belfast (Good Friday) Agreement

Although the Agreement is non-justiciable in its own right, a large proportion of its content has been put on a legislative basis and the totality of its content is capable of having some legal effects in domestic law via the principle of legality, which holds that the UK Parliament will be presumed by the courts to legislate compatibly with its international law obligations unless it clearly indicates that it intends not to.[1] Perhaps the most conspicuous case to have tested the boundaries of these legal effects is *Re Robinson's Application*, in which Peter Robinson MLA, who opposed the Agreement, challenged whether the individuals elected as First and deputy First Ministers in November 2001 could validly assume those offices as their election had taken place after the expiry of a six-week time limit provided for by section 16(8) of the Northern Ireland Act 1998. In the Court of Appeal, Nicholson LJ (with whom McCollum LJ agreed) ruled that the 1998 Act 'should be construed, if possible, so as to preserve the Belfast Agreement, not to imperil it' and that accordingly Kerr J, in the court below,[2] had been correct to adopt a purposive approach to section 16(8).[3] A majority in the House of Lords ultimately endorsed this purposive approach to the 1998 Act,[4] turning *Robinson* into a 'seminal case' on the concept

---

[1] See Conor McCormick, 'The Amendability of the Agreement' (Fortnight, Issue 489, April 2023), https://fortnightmagazine.org/artic les/the-amendability-of-the-agreement/.

[2] [2001] NIQB 49, [2002] NI 64.

[3] [2002] NICA 18, [2002] NI 206 (Carswell LCJ dissented).

[4] [2002] UKHL 32, [2002] NI 390 (two of the five Law Lords dissented).

of constitutional statutes and on the Agreement as an aid to statutory interpretation.[5]

In subsequent cases, the Court of Appeal has further refined this jurisprudence about how statutory provisions underpinned by the Agreement should be interpreted. It has adopted a mostly restrained approach, which suggests that *Robinson* set an exceptionally high watermark regarding generous and purposive statutory interpretation. In *Re Neill's Application*, for example, the Agreement's equality provisions implicitly underpinned a challenge to anti-social behaviour orders (ASBOs) and the legislation by which they had been introduced in Northern Ireland.[6] Section 75 of the Northern Ireland Act 1998 imposes a statutory duty on public authorities to have 'due regard to the need to promote equality of opportunity' between several designated groups, as required by the Agreement. In this case it was argued, *inter alia*, that the Secretary of State had failed to comply with his section 75 obligations in circumstances involving a policy more likely to affect young males than other demographics. Taking into account the wider legislative scheme of the 1998 Act, the Court of Appeal decided that procedural breaches of section 75 were non-justiciable because an alternative remedy involving the laying of a report by the Equality Commission for political consideration was provided for in Schedule 9 to the 1998 Act. By effectively foreclosing the enforcement of section 75 equality duties by way of the coercive remedies available

---

[5] Gordon Anthony, *Judicial Review in Northern Ireland* (3rd edn, Hart Publishing 2024) 21; Gordon Anthony, 'Lord Kerr and the Northern Ireland Constitution: Three Key Cases' in Brice Dickson and Conor McCormick (eds), *The Judicial Mind: A Festschrift for Lord Kerr* (Hart Publishing 2021) 90; Marie Lynch, 'Political Adjudication or Statutory Interpretation: *Robinson v Secretary of State for Northern Ireland*' (2002) 53 *NILQ* 327; Marie Lynch, '*Robinson v Secretary of State for Northern Ireland*: Interpreting Constitutional Legislation' [2003] *Public Law* 640.

[6] [2006] NICA 5, [2006] NI 278.

through a judicial review application, the decision in *Neill* has been characterised as a 'leading authority'[7] on this delimiting principle of public law.

The Court has been reluctant to provide for legal enforcement of the Agreement's provisions in other contexts too. In *Re McCord's Application*, for instance, it dismissed an appeal where the appellant unsuccessfully argued that the Secretary of State was obliged to publish a policy governing her discretionary power to hold a 'border poll' on the constitutional status of Northern Ireland, as well as a policy governing her mandatory duty to hold a border poll under certain conditions.[8] The appellant attempted to pray in aid of the Agreement and a purposive approach to the relevant statutory provisions by suggesting, for example, that published policies would 'allow political parties and individuals to democratically lobby or agitate for their preferred outcome',[9] but none of these arguments succeeded in persuading the Court to intervene.

The judicial reticence evident in decisions such as *Neill* and *McCord* can be contrasted with the Court of Appeal's approach to public law challenges taken in respect of departmental decisions made without ministerial oversight when the political institutions of devolved government envisaged by the Agreement were non-operational between 2017 and 2020. The 'landmark'[10] case of *Re Buick's Application*,[11]

---

[7] Anthony, *Judicial Review*, n 5, 152.

[8] [2020] NICA 23, [2021] NI 318.

[9] Ibid, [10].

[10] Anurag Deb, 'The Legacy of *Buick*: Northern Ireland's Chaotic Constitutional Crucible' (2019) 23(2) *Edinburgh Law Review* 259, 259; Gordon Anthony, 'The Quartet Plus Two: Judicial Review in Northern Ireland' in TT Arvind and others (eds), *Executive Decision-Making and the Courts: Revisiting the Origins of Modern Judicial Review* (Hart Publishing 2021) 261–77.

[11] [2018] NICA 26 (holding that the relevant department did not have power to grant planning permission for a major waste incinerator in the absence of a minister).

in particular, demonstrates that while the Court is generally willing to afford a wide degree of latitude to public decision-makers faced with difficult situations created by political instability, it is also prepared to issue administratively challenging judgments in order to uphold the rule of law.[12] The majority of the Court of Appeal in *Buick* still attracted some criticism for basing their findings of unlawfulness solely on the cross-cutting nature of the decision involved (which thereby breached a statutory requirement for consideration by the inoperative Executive Committee) rather than on the constitutional necessity of ministerial accountability per se.[13] In *JR80*, however, a differently constituted majority was willing to go further by condemning (though not invalidating) similarly controversial decision-making powers for civil servants that had been cloaked with the protection of Westminster legislation after *Buick*.[14] These judgments thus serve as a reminder that the Court of Appeal's weighing of constitutional principle and practicality can vary on a case-by-case basis.

---

[12] For an example arising outside the context of suspended political institutions, see *Minister for Infrastructure v Safe Electricity A&T Ltd* [2022] NICA 61, [2023] NI 348, which is criticised by Anurag Deb in 'Constitutional Amendment by Interpretive Sidewind? *Minister for Infrastructure v Safe Electricity A&T*' (UK Constitutional Law Association Blog, 7 September 2023), https://ukconstitutionallaw.org/2023/09/07/anurag-deb-constitutional-amendment-by-interpretive-sidewind-minister-for-infrastructure-v-safe-electricity-at/. See too *McKee & Hughes v The Charity Commission for Northern Ireland* [2020] NICA 13, assessed by Anurag Deb in 'Devolved Primary Legislation and the Gaze of the Common Law: A View from Northern Ireland' [2021] *Public Law* 565.

[13] For example, Deb, 'The Legacy of *Buick*', n 10, 264–5.

[14] *Re JR80's Application* [2019] NICA 58, [2021] NI 115, [109]: 'We consider that the present arrangements do not provide good governance for Northern Ireland, they are not democratic and have led to government by civil servants with only an attenuated degree of accountability.'

6.2.1.2 Brexit

McCorkindale and McHarg have observed how 'the long process of deciding whether, and if so on what terms, to leave the European Union was one marked by hyper-litigation' across the UK.[15] The same study charts how Northern Ireland was responsible for a fair share of that litigation, with some cases being commenced here but later joined with cases begun elsewhere in the UK when appealed or referred to the Supreme Court;[16] whereas other cases remained focused on Northern Ireland specific points of law throughout.[17] There has been much written about the substance of these cases already,[18] so for present purposes we only wish to observe that the Court of Appeal was involved in them to notably different extents. In *Miller/Agnew/McCord*,[19] for instance, while the Attorney General for Northern Ireland was responsible for referring four of the five questions arising from devolution proceedings in the Northern Ireland High Court to the Supreme Court, the Court of Appeal's role was largely limited to referring a fifth

---

[15] Christopher McCorkindale and Aileen McHarg, 'Litigating Brexit' in Oran Doyle, Aileen McHarg, and Jo Murkens (eds), *The Brexit Challenge for Ireland and the United Kingdom: Constitutions Under Pressure* (Cambridge University Press 2021) 260.

[16] See *R (Miller) v Secretary of State for Exiting the EU; In re McCord; In re Agnew* [2017] UKSC 5, [2018] AC 61.

[17] See *Re McCord's Application & Ors* [2019] NICA 49; *Re JR83 (No 2)* [2021] NICA 49.

[18] For example, Christopher McCrudden and Daniel Halberstam, '*Miller* and Northern Ireland: A Critical Constitutional Response' in Daniel Clarry (ed), *The UK Supreme Court Yearbook – Volume 8: Legal Year 2016–2017* (Appellate Press 2018); Gordon Anthony, 'Sovereignty, Consent, and Constitutions: The Northern Ireland References' in Mark Elliott, Jack Williams, and Alison L Young (eds), *The UK Constitution After Miller: Brexit and Beyond* (Hart Publishing 2018); Anurag Deb, 'Parliamentary Sovereignty and the Protocol Pincer' (2023) 43 *Legal Studies* 47.

[19] n 16.

question which the Attorney had ruled out as meritless.[20] In *McCord/JR83/Waring* and *JR83 (No 2)*,[21] on the other hand, the Court of Appeal issued full judgments which were not later considered by the Supreme Court (though Mr McCord did intervene in the *Miller/Cherry* case with similar arguments to those that had been raised in his own case before the Court of Appeal).[22]

More recently, the Court of Appeal has been grappling with Brexit's complicated legal consequences for Northern Ireland, primarily as manifested in the Ireland/Northern Ireland Protocol to the Withdrawal Agreement between the UK and the EU (as amended by the Windsor Framework). The most prominent case of this nature decided by the Court of Appeal thus far is *Re Allister's Application*, which was primarily about the Protocol's compatibility with various domestic law provisions of constitutional significance.[23] Both the Court of Appeal and the Supreme Court confirmed that while the Protocol had modified those constitutional provisions, it did so lawfully by way of primary legislation.[24] Following *Allister*, the Court of Appeal was soon required to clarify the legal implications flowing from Article 2 of the Protocol, under which the UK must 'ensure that no diminution of rights, safeguards or equality of opportunity' – as set out generally (albeit non-exhaustively) in a particular section of the 1998 Agreement, and in a specific list of

---

[20] For a more detailed explanation of this saga, see Brice Dickson and Conor McCormick, 'Northern Ireland Dimensions to the First Decade of the United Kingdom Supreme Court' (2020) 83 *MLR* 1133, 1162.

[21] n 17.

[22] *R (Miller) v The Prime Minister; Cherry & Ors v Advocate General for Scotland* [2019] UKSC 41, [2020] AC 373.

[23] [2022] NICA 15, [2023] NI 107. For a critical analysis, see Anurag Deb, Gary Simpson, and Gabriel Tan, 'The Union in Court, Part 2: *Allister and others v Northern Ireland Secretary* [2022] NICA 15' (2022) 73 *NILQ* 782.

[24] Ibid; [2023] UKSC 5, [2023] 2 WLR 457.

anti-discrimination Directives – 'results from its withdrawal from the [European] Union'. The first challenge to reach the Court of Appeal with Article 2 at its core involved arguments suggesting that a newly promulgated package of abortion regulations discriminated against persons with disabilities.[25] While the Court dismissed that appeal on all grounds, thereby confirming the legality of the regulations, its judgment helpfully clarified 'the six elements test' for establishing a breach of Article 2.[26] It seems likely that the Court's judgment will therefore be cited regularly in forthcoming litigation, as in the recently heard appeal against Colton J's judgment in *Re Dillon's Application & Ors*, where arguments based on Article 2 of the Protocol enabled him to disapply various provisions of the Northern Ireland Troubles (Legacy and Reconciliation) Act 2023.[27]

6.2.2 Conflict-related disputes

The Court of Appeal has heard many disputes connected to the violent sectarian conflict that plagued Northern Ireland between 1968 and 1998, including appeals which have fastened upon post-conflict laws arising from the 1998 Agreement and subsequent political accords. Under the following two sub-headings, we highlight some of the most prominent criminal and civil appeals that fall within this broadly defined category, excluding those which had human rights law arguments as their focus (these are analysed together with other human rights-based cases in the next section).

---

[25] *Re SPUC Pro-Life Ltd's Application* [2023] NICA 35.

[26] Ibid, [54].

[27] [2024] NIKB 11. Colton J also declared several provisions of the 2023 Act to be incompatible with the ECHR, but in July 2024 the new Labour government announced that it was withdrawing its appeal against that part of the judgment.

6.2.2.1 Criminal appeals

By far the most headline-grabbing of conflict-related criminal cases dealt with by the Court of Appeal in recent years is *R v Adams*.[28] Gerry Adams had appealed against his convictions for attempting to escape from detention on two occasions in 1975. The Court satisfied itself that Mr Adams's convictions were safe, but its decision was subsequently overturned by the Supreme Court.[29] The Supreme Court reached its view by reasoning that the Interim Custody Order underpinning Mr Adams's detention had been signed by a Minister of State rather than the Secretary of State, contrary to a requirement under the relevant statute, whereas the Court of Appeal's judgment had placed weight on the *Carltona* principle which recognises that a Secretary of State's powers can be exercised by junior Ministers and other officials acting in his or her name. The Supreme Court's reasoning has been subjected to heavy criticism from several quarters,[30] and while its harshest critics have praised the Court of Appeal for reaching a different conclusion by reference to the *Carltona* principle, the Court of Appeal has also been attacked for permitting the appeal to proceed out of time on the basis of public records disclosed under the 30-year rule.[31] The critical response was strong enough to result in sections 46 and 47 of the Northern Ireland Troubles (Legacy and Reconciliation) Act 2023, which are essentially intended to override the Supreme Court's decision on the lawfulness of

---

[28] [2018] NICA 8.

[29] [2020] UKSC 19, [2020] 1 WLR 2077.

[30] For example, Richard Ekins and Stephen Laws, *Mishandling the Law: Gerry Adams and the Supreme Court* (Policy Exchange, 30 May 2020), https://policyexchange.org.uk/publication/mishandling-the-law/. See too Claire Archbold, 'Beyond Carltona: *R v Adams*, Accountability and the Delegation of Powers' in Dickson and McCormick (eds), *The Judicial Mind*, n 5, 243–60.

[31] Ibid, Ekins and Laws, 15.

any convictions associated with or akin to Mr Adams's and to retroactively prohibit any civil claims that might otherwise arise from them.[32] However, it should be noted that in the recently decided High Court case of *Re Dillon's Application & Ors*, those provisions, in so far as they prohibited claims made before the relevant provisions of the 2023 Act were commenced, were declared incompatible with Article 6 (the right to a fair trial) and Article 1 of Protocol 1 (protection of property) of the ECHR, though not disapplied for being inconsistent with Article 2 of the Ireland/Northern Ireland Protocol.[33]

There are at least two more criminal appeals which have generated considerable interest among local journalists and the Northern Ireland public more broadly. In *R v Gordon*, the Court of Appeal concluded that a jury's guilty verdict which had been returned in 1952 regarding the killing of Patricia Curran was not safe because the appellant's confession should not have been admitted as evidence in the trial for her murder.[34] On this basis, the jury's finding was quashed, albeit only after many years of stigmatised detention and disgrace for the appellant. The Court's judgment attracted a particularly large measure of interest because of the enduring miscarriage of justice at its centre and also, in part, because of the murder victim's status as the daughter of Sir Lancelot Curran, who had been a High Court judge at the time of her murder and subsequently became a Lord Justice of Appeal.[35]

---

[32] The Court of Appeal allowed appeals by two individuals who assisted Mr Adams with his attempted escapes from detention in 1975: *R v Bell* [2021] NICA 52 and [2021] NICA 56; *R v O'Rawe* [2021] NICA 57.

[33] n 27, [649]-[709]; see also *Re Adams's Application* [2024] NICA 15 and *Re Bannon's Application* [2024] NIKB 25. The government has since withdrawn its appeal against this part of Colton J's judgment as well.

[34] [2000] NICA 28 (not strictly conflict-related).

[35] See, for example, Freya McClements, 'Patricia Curran: The murder that is still unsolved 70 years later' (*The Irish Times*, 12 November 2022), www.irishtimes.com/culture/books/2022/11/12/murdered-teenager-patricia-curran-the-classic-noir-heroine-the-judges-daughter/.

In *R v Stone*, the Court of Appeal considered an appeal by
Michael Stone against his convictions for various criminal
offences in 2008, including two counts of attempted murder
and the possession of explosive substances with intent.[36] He
had been apprehended at the entrance to Parliament Buildings
at Stormont by security personnel. When interviewed he said
that he 'had gone to Stormont specifically to assassinate Adams
and McGuinness and to disrupt [an] event which could have
betrayed Ulster with some unionists voting to share power
with Sinn Féin',[37] but he nonetheless sought to have his
convictions quashed on the outlandish basis that, *inter alia*, he
had been 'engaged in performance art work'.[38] The Court
of Appeal was not persuaded and held that the convictions
were safe.[39] A newspaper reported that while the appellant
'sat impassively throughout the judgment after being escorted
into court on a walking stick', on his way out he shouted,
'the truth will out, gentlemen, believe me'.[40] The courage
which must be required of the Court in the face of such
dangerous characters is perhaps not as widely recognised as it
should be.

6.2.2.2 Civil appeals

The broad range of civil appeals that have reached the Court
of Appeal in connection with conflict-related matters can be

---

[36] [2011] NICA 1.

[37] Ibid, [10].

[38] Ibid, [13].

[39] Mr Stone was later involved in other appeals challenging sentences
relating to separate offences he committed against mourners at Milltown
Cemetery in 1988: *Re McGuinness's Application (No 1)* [2020] NICA 54
and *(No 3)* [2020] NICA 53.

[40] 'Court rejects Michael Stone's appeal over Stormont murder bids' (*The
Belfast Telegraph*, 7 January 2011), www.belfasttelegraph.co.uk/news/
northern-ireland/court-rejects-michael-stones-appeal-over-stormont-
murder-bids/28580271.html.

further sub-divided into two categories: tort claims and judicial review applications.

Mallory, Molloy, and Murray have argued that tort claims can be utilised not just as a means of obtaining injunctive relief and compensation but also as an incidental means of 'truth recovery'.[41] In their 2020 paper at least two notable Court of Appeal decisions were highlighted. First, they referred to the high-profile case of *Breslin & Ors v McKevitt & Ors*, which concerned several actions for damages resulting from trespasses to the person in respect of deaths and injuries caused by the appellants who, as members of the Real IRA, were allegedly responsible for the Omagh bombing on 15 August 1998.[42] The authors drew attention to '[t]he perception that a greater level of wrongfulness is inherent where a trespass to the person is established, by comparison to negligence, [which] increases its attractiveness to claimants seeking to emphasise the defendant's blameworthiness'.[43] Second, the authors highlighted *Flynn v Chief Constable of Northern Ireland* as a 'pathfinder case' in which the Court of Appeal declined to interfere with an extensive order for discovery in the court below, which the Chief Constable objected to on the bases that he had made an admission of liability rendering it unnecessary and that it was disproportionate.[44] Mallory, Molloy, and Murray credit the case for demonstrating how the discovery process in civil litigation could be used (and resisted) 'because of its potential as a mechanism for truth recovery'.[45]

The subject matter of conflict-related judicial review applications over the past 25 years has been nothing if not

---

[41] Conall Mallory, Sean Molloy, and CRG Murray, 'Tort, Truth Recovery and the Northern Ireland Conflict' [2020] 3 *EHRLR* 243.

[42] [2011] NICA 33. See also [2011] NICA 69 and [2013] NICA 75.

[43] Mallory, Molloy, and Murray, n 41, 254.

[44] [2017] NICA 13. See also [2018] NICA 3.

[45] Mallory, Molloy, and Murray, n 41, 257.

diverse. Some cases have involved challenges to significant public appointments, such as *Re Downe's Application*, which concerned a partly successful appeal from the judgment of Girvan J, whereby he granted judicial review of the decision of the then Secretary of State for Northern Ireland, Peter Hain MP, appointing Mrs Bertha McDougall as the Interim Victims Commissioner.[46] The Court of Appeal allowed the appeal against Girvan J's reasoning but decided that the Secretary of State had failed to take into account a relevant consideration; namely, the requirement that he have regard to the relevant Code of Practice in making the appointment. Because of that failure, the Court held that Mrs McDougall's appointment was unlawful and made a declaration to that effect.

Other conflict-related judicial review applications have involved further decisions made by the Secretary of State for Northern Ireland. In *Re Williamson's Application*, for instance, an appeal was dismissed in respect of a ministerial decision not to specify the Provisional IRA under section 3(8) of the Northern Ireland (Sentences) Act 1998 Act, on the ground that it was not maintaining a complete and unequivocal ceasefire.[47] If the Provisional IRA had been so specified, one of the people responsible for killing the parents of the applicant would no longer have qualified for early release from prison. The case has been characterised as one which suggested 'a judicial reluctance to become involved in high-profile political disputes' in the early aftermath of the 1998 Agreement, with the 'signals' it gave being interpreted as one reason why some of the most controversial issues of the day were not taken before the courts at all.[48] The same disinclination to interfere

---

[46] [2009] NICA 26.

[47] [2000] NICA 7, [2000] NI 281.

[48] John Morison and Marie Lynch, 'Litigating the Agreement: Towards a New Judicial Constitutionalism for the UK from Northern Ireland?' in John Morison, Kieran McEvoy, and Gordon Anthony (eds), *Judges, Transition and Human Rights* (Oxford University Press 2007) 130–1.

with controversial decisions reached by public decision-makers can be discerned in various cases involving issues laden with heightened sensitivity in Northern Ireland, such as parades,[49] flags,[50] bonfires,[51] and citizenship.[52]

6.3 Human rights cases

Given the legacy of the troubles and the persistent community tensions evident in many of the cases mentioned previously, it was inevitable that appellate judges would be required to apply a human rights lens to a multiplicity of disputes after the 1998 Agreement.[53] This section surveys some of the most notable conflict-related human rights cases decided by the Court of Appeal over the last 25 years, together with some non-conflict-related cases determined by the Court with reference to the same provisions of human rights law.

---

[49] For example, the numerous cases taken by David Tweed of Dunloy Loyal Orange Lodge 496: [2000] NICA 24; [2005] NICA 42; [2009] NICA 13. See too *Re Farrell's Application* [1999] NICA 7, [1999] NIJB 143; *Re McConnell's Application* [1999] NICA 9; *Re Pelan's Application* [2001] NICA 35; *Re Duffy's Application* [2006] NICA 28; *Re DB's Application* [2014] NICA 56, [2016] NIJB 118, overturned by the Supreme Court in *DB v Chief Constable of the Police Service of Northern Ireland* [2017] UKSC 7, [2017] NI 301; *PPS v Bryson* [2016] NICA 11.

[50] For example, *Re McMahon's Application* [2019] NICA 29; *Re McShane's Application* [2019] NICA 69, [2021] NI 161.

[51] For example, *Re Bryson's Application* [2022] NICA 38.

[52] For example, *Re Ní Chuinneagain's Application* [2022] NICA 56.

[53] For a concise analysis of how human rights were given effect by the courts of Northern Ireland before and after 1998, see Ronagh McQuigg, 'A "Very Limited" Effect or a "Seismic" Impact? A Study of the Impact of the Human Rights Act 1998 on the Courts of Northern Ireland' [2010] *Public Law* 551. For a broader analysis of the ECHR in this context, see Brice Dickson, *The European Convention on Human Rights and the Conflict in Northern Ireland* (Oxford University Press 2010).

6.3.1 Articles 2 and 3 of the ECHR

In no context was a human rights lens more apparent than that of the investigation of troubles-related killings. A recurring question was whether the investigative duty under Article 2 required such killings to be investigated in an ECHR-compliant way even though Convention rights became part of domestic law only on 2 October 2000, when the Human Rights Act came fully into force. In *Re McKerr's Application*, a case where the High Court answered no to that question, the Court of Appeal disagreed.[54] On a further appeal, however, the House of Lords ruled that the Human Rights Act did not have that retrospective effect.[55] Some six years later, in *Re McCaughey's Application*,[56] the Court of Appeal acknowledged that the European Court, in *Šilih v Slovenia*, had meanwhile stated that the investigative duty was a free-standing right which could apply to killings occurring up to ten years before the ECHR became binding on the country in question.[57] Nevertheless, the Court of Appeal felt obliged to apply the House of Lords precedent in *McKerr*. Then four of the seven Supreme Court Justices who heard a further appeal in *McCaughey* reversed the Court of Appeal, while not expressly overruling the House of Lords ruling in *McKerr*.[58] It seemed that the Court of Appeal just could not get it right!

Prior to the same issue confronting the Court yet again, European judges decided *Brecknell v UK*, ruling that even if an investigation of a killing took place more than ten years before 'the crucial date', the duty to investigate could be 'revived' if certain conditions were fulfilled.[59] In no fewer than four

---

[54] [2003] NICA 1, [2003] NI 117.

[55] [2004] UKHL 12, [2004] 1 WLR 807, relying on s 22(4) of the Act.

[56] [2010] NICA 13.

[57] (2009) 49 EHRR 37.

[58] [2004] UKHL 12, [2004] 1 WLR 807.

[59] (2008) 46 EHRR 42. For judges in the ECtHR 'the crucial date' is 14 January 1966, when the UK first allowed individuals to lodge applications

further cases the Court of Appeal duly held that Article 2 did require an effective investigation: *Finucane v Secretary of State for Northern Ireland*,[60] *Re McQuillan's Application*,[61] *Re Barnard's Application*,[62] and *Re Dalton's Application*.[63] In a fifth case, *Re McGuigan's Application*, which raised Article 3 issues (the prohibition of torture), the Court held that the 'revival' test was not satisfied, although by a majority it also ruled that the Chief Constable had created a legitimate expectation that an ECHR-compliant investigation would be conducted.[64] Four of those five cases were appealed to the Supreme Court.[65] The appeal was dismissed in *Finucane* and *McGuigan*, with an acceptance in *Finucane* that the investigative duty should apply even though the killing occurred as many as 12 years before 2 October 2000.[66] In *McQuillan* and *Dalton* the Supreme Court reversed the Court of Appeal on the basis that the killings had occurred too long ago, even though Mr Dalton was killed just two months before the cut-off point and less than six months before Mr Finucane's killing.[67]

Throughout the past 25 years the Court has dealt on no fewer than ten occasions with litigation brought by the family of Pearse Jordan, an unarmed IRA volunteer shot dead by the

---

in Strasbourg; for judges in the UK it is 2 October 2000, when the Human Rights Act 1998 came fully into force in domestic law.

[60] [2017] NICA 7.

[61] [2019] NICA 13, [2020] NI 583.

[62] [2019] NICA 38.

[63] [2020] NICA 26, [2021] NI 405.

[64] [2019] NICA 46, [2021] NI 15.

[65] The exception was *Barnard's Application*.

[66] *Re Geraldine Finucane's Application* [2019] UKSC 7, [2019] 3 All ER 191; *Re Francis McGuigan's Application* [2021] UKSC 55, [2022] AC 1063.

[67] *Re Margaret McQuillan's Application* [2021] UKSC 55, [2022] AC 1063; *Re Rosaleen Dalton's Application* [2023] UKSC 36, [2023] 3 WLR 671. For highly critical commentary on the Supreme Court's *McQuillan* judgment, see Anurag Deb and Colin Murray, 'Sealing the Past: *McQuillan* and the Future of Legacy Litigation' [2022] *EHRLR* 395.

police in 1992.[68] A whole book could be written about that litigation but for present purposes it suffices to note that the cases often required the Court to decide what exactly an Article 2-compliant investigation entails. One such case was appealed unsuccessfully to the House of Lords, where by three to two the Lords confirmed that inquests in Northern Ireland could not return verdicts of lawful or unlawful killing.[69] Another was appealed successfully to the Supreme Court, which held unanimously that payment of compensation for delay in holding an Article 2-compliant inquest should not have to await the completion of that inquest.[70]

The Court of Appeal has wrestled with Article 2 of the ECHR in other contexts too. In *Re Meehan's Application* it agreed that a refusal to grant a firearm certificate to a former IRA member should not be interfered with because the applicant had not demonstrated a real and immediate risk to his life.[71] In *Re Officer L's Application* it upheld Morgan J's decision that the public inquiry into the murder of Robert Hamill should not have granted anonymity to serving and retired police officers when giving evidence at the inquiry,[72] but on appeal the House of Lords said the Court had applied the wrong test under Article 2 and it restored the inquiry's original decision on the matter.[73] In *Re A's Application* the Court did grant anonymity to former members of the Royal

---

[68] *Re Jordan's Applications* [2002] NICA 27; [2003] NICA 30, [2004] NIJB 42; [2003] NICA 54, [2004] NI 198; [2004] NICA 29/30, [2005] NI 144; [2009] NICA 64; [2014] NICA 36, [2016] NI 107; [2014] NICA 76, [2016] NI 116; [2015] NICA 66; [2018] NICA 23, [2020] NIJB 296; [2018] NICA 34.

[69] *Jordan v Lord Chancellor* [2007] UKHL 14, [2007] AC 226, on appeal from [2004] NICA 29/30.

[70] *Re Jordan's Application* [2019] UKSC 9, [2020] NI 570, on appeal from [2015] NICA 66.

[71] [2004] NICA 34, [2004] NIJB 53.

[72] [2007] NICA 8.

[73] [2007] UKHL 36, [2007] 1 WLR 2135.

Irish Regiment who were giving evidence at an inquiry into the murder of a solicitor, Rosemary Nelson.[74] A claim by Iris Robinson, the wife of the then First Minister of Northern Ireland, that the hearing of her defamation action against a Sunday newspaper should be held in private because of the risk to her life given her serious mental condition, was also accepted by the Court of Appeal.[75] Moreover, returning to investigative obligations, in *Re McEvoy's Application* the Court upheld a compensatory award of £10,000 against the police for their failure to ensure an ECHR-compliant investigation into a shooting incident in which the applicant was injured.[76]

Article 3 featured in the failed attempt by the Northern Ireland Human Rights Commission to convince the Court of Appeal that police were endangering children by not properly controlling protestors who were seriously harassing those children on their way to school.[77] The House of Lords and the European Court endorsed that view.[78] In *Re NICCY's Application* the Court rejected an argument that parental chastisement of their children was a breach of Article 3.[79]

---

[74] [2009] NICA 6.

[75] *Robinson v Sunday Newspapers Ltd* [2011] NICA 13. See too *King v Sunday Newspapers Ltd* [2011] NICA 8, [2012] NI 1, where on Art 2 and 3 grounds the claimant succeeded in preventing a newspaper from identifying his partner.

[76] [2023] NICA 66.

[77] *Re E's Application* [2006] NICA 37, [2007] NIJB 189.

[78] *E v Chief Constable of the RUC* [2008] UKHL 66, [2009] 1 AC 536; *PF and EF v UK* App 28326/09, 23 November 2010, [2011] *EHRLR* 213. In a later case the Supreme Court overruled a Court of Appeal decision that the police were correct not to try to stop 'flag' protests, because of potential repercussions elsewhere: the Art 11 right to freedom of assembly and association was subordinated to the Art 8 right to a private and family life: *DB*, n 49.

[79] [2009] NICA 10, [2009] NI 235 (though its main ruling was that the Commissioner for Children and Young People had no legal standing to bring the case).

6.3.2 Other ECHR Articles

In relation to Article 6 of the ECHR (the right to a fair trial), the Court refused compensation to an applicant whose conviction it had previously quashed in line with a judgment of the European Court of Human Rights that his trial had been unfair.[80] Years later it also denied compensation to a couple who had been wrongly convicted of allowing property to be used for terrorist purposes.[81] The ECHR does not require compensation to be paid merely because a breach of Article 6 has occurred: the declaration of a breach is sometimes considered 'adequate satisfaction'.

Defendants in criminal trials frequently complain about the prosecution's failure to disclose evidence which might help the defence, but in *R v McKeown* the Court of Appeal was not persuaded that there had been such a failure.[82] On the other hand, in *R v Higgins*, an appeal against a confiscation order for a sum exceeding £16,000, the Court found a breach of Article 6 '[i]n view of the combination of procedural errors and shortcomings, the protracted delays and the discharge of counsel in circumstances in which the applicant should have had the benefit of legal assistance'.[83]

Prisoners have been frequent litigants in the Court of Appeal. One issue has been whether revocation of a prisoner's early release date is lawful. In *Re McClean's Application* the applicant failed to convince the Court that an amendment to the Northern Ireland (Sentences) Act 1998 (allowing for the early release of prisoners) was in violation of either Article 5 of the ECHR (the right to liberty) or Article 6.[84] The decision

---

[80] *Re Magee's Application* [2007] NICA 34; *Magee v UK* (2001) 31 EHRR 35.

[81] *Re Ryan's Application* [2021] NICA 42. The Supreme Court refused leave to appeal.

[82] [2004] NICA 41, [2005] NI 301, [42] per Girvan LJ.

[83] [2014] NICA 47, [2016] NI 1, citing *Anderson v UK*, App 19859/04, 9 February 2010.

[84] [2004] NICA 14, [2005] NI 1 (on Art 5); [2004] NICA 13, [2005] NI 21 (on Art 6).

by Sentence Review Commissioners did not even engage Article 6 because it did not involve the determination of a 'civil right', but the Court did rule (Higgins LJ dissenting) that the Commissioners needed to reconsider McClean's position because they had wrongly placed on him the burden of proving that he would not be a danger to the public if released immediately. In a later case the Court held that Life Sentence Review Commissioners had breached Article 5(4) of the ECHR by not dealing with a prisoner's application speedily enough.[85]

In *R v Morgan* four prisoners complained that their sentences for terrorist offences had been unlawfully extended by a legislative amendment, in breach of Article 7 of the ECHR (no punishment without law).[86] The Court declared the amendment to be incompatible with the ECHR, thinking it was adhering to the Supreme Court's approach to Article 7, but on appeal the Supreme Court ruled that the amendment did not modify the sentence but merely changed its manner of execution.[87] Both courts were referred to all relevant case law from Strasbourg, but while the Court of Appeal concluded that the amendment effectively breached the rule of law,[88] the Supreme Court viewed it as not falling within the concept of 'law' at all.[89] In a different case, where a prisoner argued that a new scheme meant he would receive less home leave than before, the Court found that his Article 8 rights (the right to respect for a private and family life) had been breached.[90] Likewise, in *Re Conway's Application* the Court remitted a case to the High Court so that an assessment could be made

---

[85] *R v Mullan* [2007] NICA 47, [2008] NI 258.

[86] [2021] NICA 67. Art 20A was inserted into the Criminal Justice (NI) Order 2008 by s 30 of the Counter Terrorism and Sentencing Act 2021.

[87] [2023] UKSC 14, [2024] AC 130.

[88] n 86, [95].

[89] n 87, [117].

[90] *Re Griffin's Application* [2005] NICA 15, [2006] NIJB 56.

of whether the policy of conducting full-body searches on prisoners entering and leaving a prison was flexible enough to avoid breaching Article 8 in particular cases.[91]

The Court has also considered Article 8 in a variety of other contexts, such as objecting to planning permission for a building beside the applicant's home,[92] challenging the Housing Executive's refusal to evict a tenant who was harassing his neighbours,[93] establishing a claim to a widowed parent's allowance,[94] and complaining about discrimination against a gay couple who wanted to marry.[95] In that last arena the Court said that current legislation on marriage did not strike a fair balance between tradition and personal rights and it emphasised that 'where the petition of concern is utilised to defeat the will of the Assembly on an issue dealing with a difference of treatment on the grounds of sexual orientation the scrutiny required by the courts is enhanced'.[96] The Court displayed a rather conservative stance when it ruled that the ban on unmarried couples adopting children was lawful: the Supreme Court put them right on that matter[97] and the Court of Appeal

---

[91] [2012] NICA 11, [2013] NI 102.

[92] *Re Stewart's Application* [2003] NICA 4, [2003] NI 149 (no breach of Art 8 or of Art 1 of Protocol 1 (protection of property)).

[93] *Re Donnelly's Application* [2003] NICA 55, [2004] NI 189 (breach of Art 8).

[94] *Re McLaughlin's Application* [2016] NICA 53 (no breach of Art 8, taken together with Art 14 (prohibition of discrimination)), but the Supreme Court reversed the Court of Appeal: [2018] UKSC 48, [2018] 1 WLR 4250.

[95] *Re Close's Application* [2020] NICA 20, [2021] NI 276. See too *Re X's Petition* [2020] NICA 21, on the recognition of same-sex marriages conducted in England and Wales. For a complimentary appraisal of the Court of Appeal's approach to these cases, see Conor McCormick and Thomas Stewart, 'The Legalisation of Same-Sex Marriage in Northern Ireland' (2020) 71 *NILQ* 557, 566–9.

[96] Ibid, [54] per Morgan LCJ.

[97] *Re P (A Child)* [2007] NICA 20, [2007] NI 251, on appeal as *In re G (Adoption: Unmarried Couple)* [2008] UKHL 38, [2009] 1 AC 173.

later applied that precedent in *Re NIHRC's Application*, which related to adoption by a gay couple.[98] It also ruled in favour of a man who claimed sexual orientation discrimination when a bakery refused to decorate a cake he had ordered with the words 'Support Gay Marriage'.[99] Controversially, the Supreme Court allowed the bakery's appeal. It is arguable that in doing so it failed to take full account of Northern Ireland's discrete laws on political opinion discrimination.[100]

Article 8 was cited in three important cases on abortion, where the Court has been moderately activist. In *Re Family Planning Association's Application* it declared that the Minister for Health had failed to comply with her statutory obligation to issue guidance to women and clinicians on the availability of pregnancy termination services.[101] On the other hand, in *Attorney General for Northern Ireland v Northern Ireland Human Rights Commission* it held that criminalising abortion did not breach Article 8 even in cases of pregnancy caused by rape or incest or resulting in a fatal foetal abnormality.[102] Subsequent regulations providing for abortion were challenged by the Society for the Protection of the Unborn Child as being beyond the Secretary of State's law-making powers, but the Court dismissed that claim.[103]

---

[98] [2013] NICA 37.

[99] *Lee v McArthur* [2016] NICA 39.

[100] *Lee v Ashers Baking Company Ltd* [2018] UKSC 49, [2020] AC 413; for a full critique, see Brice Dickson, 'The "Gay Cake" Case and the Scope of Discrimination Law' in Daniel Clarry (ed), *The UK Supreme Court Yearbook – Volume 10: Legal Year 2018–2019* (Appellate Press 2021).

[101] [2004] NICA 37–39, [2005] NI 188.

[102] [2017] NICA 42. Morgan LCJ thought that current law permitted abortion in such cases. On appeal the Supreme Court ruled that the NIHRC had no legal standing to bring the case but let it be known (by a majority) that Art 8 is breached if no abortion is available in situations of rape, incest, or fatal foetal abnormality: *Re NIHRC's Application* [2008] UKSC 27, [2019] 1 All ER 173.

[103] n 25.

Occasionally the Court has taken what might appear to be unjust decisions but has justified them by indicating it was merely applying the will of legislators, on whom the responsibility for any required reform lies. For instance, in a case concerning access to welfare benefits by persons suffering from serious progressive illnesses the Court emphasised that 'considerable weight should be given to the views of the primary decision maker' and that it had been confronted with choices which were 'for the political process and not for the courts'.[104] Furthermore, in *Re Misbehavin' Ltd's Application* it tried to ensure that Belfast City Council took account of Article 10 of the ECHR (freedom of expression) when deciding whether to grant an application for a sex establishment licence by faithfully applying the Human Rights Act 1998.[105] But on appeal the House of Lords held that it did not matter whether a public authority took account of human rights standards when reaching decisions so long as no such rights were actually breached by the decision taken.[106]

In relation to Article 14 of the ECHR and Article 1 of Protocol 1 the Court of Appeal has frequently balanced human rights against other interests without being appealed against.[107] But it was overturned in two cases dealing respectively with entitlement to a pension and a welfare benefit: *Re Brewster's Application*[108] and *Re McLaughlin's Application.*[109]

---

[104] *Department for Communities v Cox* [2021] NICA 46, [2022] NI 235, [75].

[105] [2005] NICA 35, [2006] NI 181.

[106] [2007] UKHL, [2007] 1 WLR 1420.

[107] For example, *Re Meehan's Application* [2018] NICA 42, [2020] NI 440; *O'Donnell v Department for Communities* [2020] NICA 36, [2021] NI 490; *Re Renewable Heat Association's Application* [2023] NICA 13, [2023] NI 363.

[108] [2013] NICA 54; [2017] UKSC 8, [2017] 1 WLR 519.

[109] [2016] NICA 53; [2018] UKSC 48, [2018] 1 WLR 4250.

6.4 Conclusion

This chapter has laid out some of the most memorable and impactful Court of Appeal cases that have been determined over the past quarter of a century. It has shown that while nuanced critiques orbit the Court's judgments to a healthy degree, whether as a result of being appealed to the top of the judicial hierarchy or on account of non-judicial commentary,[110] the work of the Court has also prompted praise from time to time.[111] Most of the Court's judgments in this space are undoubtedly laced with a notable level of deference to other public decision-makers and by a subtle tendency to favour pragmatic solutions. Naturally, opinions will differ on the extent to which greater judicial activism might be ideologically justified.

---

[110] See, for example, n 70 and n 13 respectively.

[111] See, for example, n 30 and n 95.

SEVEN

Appeals to the House of Lords and the Supreme Court

7.1 Introduction

While judges in intermediate appeal courts must be constantly conscious of the fact that they are, in effect, judging the judges who work below them in the court hierarchy, they must be thinking from time to time that their own judgments might soon be closely scrutinised by judges above them in that hierarchy. This chapter surveys the frequency, and success rate, of appeals from rulings of the Court of Appeal to the House of Lords and (since October 2009) the Supreme Court. It begins by clarifying the circumstances in which appeals (or references) might reach the top court, then looks at the number, outcomes, and subject matter of appeals and finally analyses how the judgments of the various Chief Justices of Northern Ireland have fared when they have been considered in London.[1]

7.2 The appeal routes

Prior to the formation of the United Kingdom of Great Britain and Ireland in 1801, appeals from courts in Ireland had

---

[1] Initial parts of this chapter rely to some extent on Brice Dickson, 'Northern Ireland after 1921' in Louis Blom-Cooper, Brice Dickson, and Gavin Drewry (eds), *The Judicial House of Lords 1876–2009* (Oxford University Press 2009) 304–14.

sometimes gone to the English House of Lords in London and sometimes to the Irish House of Lords in Dublin, but the Act of Union 1800 made it clear that thereafter all appeals would be heard only by the former of those institutions. In 1876, Lords of Appeal in Ordinary were specially appointed to hear all appeals in the House of Lords. Although a High Court of Appeal in Ireland was in place for almost a year in 1921–22, serving as an intermediate court between the two Courts of Appeal in Northern Ireland and Southern Ireland and the House of Lords,[2] the latter continued as the apex court in the Northern Ireland legal system until it was superseded by the Supreme Court in October 2009.[3] Only in 1962 did it become necessary in nearly every case for leave to appeal to the House of Lords to be granted prior to the lodging of an appeal.[4]

Today an appeal from a decision of the Court of Appeal relating to a criminal case heard by the Crown Court can be taken by either the defendant or the prosecutor to the Supreme Court,[5] but no such appeal is possible unless the Court of Appeal first certifies that a point of law of general public importance is involved and the Court of Appeal or the Supreme Court then grants leave on the basis that the point is one which ought to be considered by the Supreme Court.[6] There is also a right of appeal from a decision of the Court of Appeal in a criminal cause or matter upon a case stated by a county court or a magistrates' court, subject to the same preconditions.[7]

An appeal from a decision of the Court of Appeal in a civil case also requires either the Court of Appeal or the Supreme

---

[2] See Chapter 2.

[3] The appeal route was confirmed by the Northern Ireland Act 1962, s 1 and again by the Judicature (NI) Act 1978, ss 40–3.

[4] Northern Ireland Act 1962, s 1(2).

[5] Criminal Appeal (NI) Act 1980, s 31(1).

[6] Ibid, s 31(6).

[7] Judicature (NI) Act 1978, ss 41(1)(b) and 41(2).

Court to grant permission for the appeal, but there is no requirement for the Court of Appeal to certify that a point of law of general public importance is involved.[8] However in a case where by statute it is expressly provided that the Court of Appeal's order or judgment is to be final, no appeal is possible unless it involves a decision as to the validity of any provision made by or under an Act of the Parliament of Northern Ireland or a Measure of the Northern Ireland Assembly.[9]

In both criminal and civil cases it is now very rare for the Court of Appeal to grant leave to appeal since it is accepted that the Supreme Court prefers to have the final say over which appeals it hears.[10] An example of the Court of Appeal granting leave in a civil case occurred in 2019 when it gave leave to the unsuccessful applicants in a judicial review of the Ireland/Northern Ireland Protocol to the EU–UK Withdrawal Agreement.[11]

It is also possible for cases from Northern Ireland to reach the Supreme Court without first having been heard by the Court of Appeal, most notably when the Divisional Court of the High Court has made a decision in a judicial review involving a criminal cause or matter.[12] Both in Northern

---

[8] Judicature (NI) Act 1978, s 42(1) and (2). In Ireland Art $34.5.3^0$ of the Constitution provides that only the Supreme Court can grant leave for an appeal from the Court of Appeal (whether in a criminal or civil case) and such leave can be granted only if the Supreme Court is satisfied either that the decision involves a matter of general public importance or that it is necessary in the interests of justice that there be an appeal.

[9] Ibid, s 42(6).

[10] See, for example, *G Hamilton (Tullochgribban Mains) Ltd v The Highland Council* [2012] UKSC 31, 2013 SC (UKSC) 45; *Kinloch v HM Advocate* [2012] UKSC 62, [2013] 2 AC 93.

[11] *Re Allister's Application* [2023] UKSC 5, [2023] 2 WLR 457. A further example is *In re McCaughey* [2011] UKSC 20, [2012] 1 AC 725.

[12] Judicature (NI) Act 1978, s 41(1)(a); a comparable appeal route exists in England and Wales under the Administration of Justice Act 1960, s 1(1)(a). Strangely, the first such appeal in Northern Ireland did not occur until 2007. To date there have been nine.

Ireland and in England and Wales there is also the possibility of a 'leapfrog appeal' from the High Court directly to the House of Lords or Supreme Court. It can occur if all parties to the case consent to it and if the appeal raises a question of law of general public importance involving either the interpretation of a piece of legislation or an issue on which the High Court is bound by a previous decision of a higher court.[13] Finally, issues can reach the Supreme Court if they are 'referred' to that Court. The Court of Appeal in Northern Ireland can itself refer to the Supreme Court any devolution issue which arises in proceedings before it[14] and the Attorney General and the Advocate General for Northern Ireland can do so too – even without first giving the Court of Appeal an opportunity to look at the matter – when there is a question whether a provision in a Bill would be within the legislative competence of the Northern Ireland Assembly.[15]

7.3 Applications for leave to appeal

Thanks to the assistance of the Court of Appeal Office, we have had access to previously unpublished statistics concerning applications for leave to appeal from the Court of Appeal. They are set out in Table 7.1.

---

[13] Administration of Justice Act 1969, ss 12–16. No such leapfrog appeal has yet occurred in Northern Ireland. No appeal lies against a refusal by the High Court to issue a certificate stating that no question of law of general public importance arises in a case (Judicature (NI) Act 1978, s 35(2)(i)); there appears to be no equivalent provision in England and Wales.

[14] Northern Ireland Act 1998, Sch 10, para 9. For the only example, see the reference made by the Court of Appeal in *R (Miller) v Secretary of State for Exiting the European Union* [2017] UKSC 5, [2018] AC 61, where an additional four references were made by the High Court of Northern Ireland at the insistence of the Attorney General using his powers under Sch 10, para 33.

[15] Ibid, s 11. Three such references have been made since 1999.

Table 7.1: Applications to the Court of Appeal for leave to appeal to the House of Lords or Supreme Court disposed of, 2007–23

	Civil cases	Criminal cases	Total cases
2007	15	3	18
2008	13	4	17
2009	7	1	8
2010	11	2	13
2011	15	8	23
2012	28	4	32
2013	29	6	35
2014	28	8	36
2015	14	10	24
2016	24	3	27
2017	55	4	59
2018	13	6	19
2019	28	4	32
2020	13	8	21
2021	13	7	20
2022	30	13	43
2023	35	1	36
Total	371	92	463
Average per year	22	5	27

It can be seen that on the civil side the figures tend to differ significantly from year to year and that overall there were four times as many applications in civil cases as in criminal cases. Unfortunately, the Court of Appeal Office was not able to say how many applications resulted in leave being granted, or how many applications in criminal cases resulted at least in the identification of a question of law of general public importance. We also do not know how many unsuccessful applications were resubmitted to the Supreme Court and whether they were successful there. The Supreme Court's Annual Reports no longer specify from which jurisdiction in the UK applications for permission to appeal derive, but from analysing the 'PTA' decisions listed on the Court's website up to the end of 2023 we calculate that since the Supreme Court's establishment in 2009 there have been 168 applications from Northern Ireland, 40 of which were granted (24 per cent). Of those, 33 related to appeals from the Court of Appeal and seven to appeals from the Divisional Court. Since 2009, therefore, there have been on average two or three successful applications per year in respect of decisions taken by the Court of Appeal.

Currently all applications to the Court of Appeal for leave to appeal to the Supreme Court are dealt with at an oral hearing. The Report of the Civil Justice Review in 2017 pointed out that this was time-consuming and generated costs[16] and it therefore recommended that in future all such applications should be made in writing and decided by the issue of an Order, with an oral hearing taking place only when considered necessary.[17] The same Report observed that the test applied by the Court of Appeal for granting leave was out of step with the Supreme Court's test. The Court of Appeal grants leave if there is a conflict of authority at the domestic level or with European authority, whereas the Supreme Court grants leave if the application raises 'an arguable point of law of general public importance which ought to be considered by the Supreme Court at that time, bearing in mind that the

---

[16] Report of the Review on Civil Justice (2017), para 15.25.

[17] Ibid, para 15.59 and Recommendation CJ133. The Report noted that in England and Wales such applications can be dealt with purely on the basis of written submissions.

matter will already have been the subject of judicial decision and may have already been reviewed on appeal'.[18] The Report recommended that the Court of Appeal should change its practice accordingly.[19]

It appears that these recommendations by the Civil Justice Review have not yet been formally implemented. The Practice Direction governing procedures in the Court of Appeal makes no mention of how to apply to the Supreme Court,[20] but in our interviews with several judges who have sat on the Court of Appeal,[21] we discovered that most of them believe the Court of Appeal should grant leave to the Supreme Court 'sparingly'.[22] We heard that this approach was justified because 'the Supreme Court should be in charge of its own docket'.[23] Interestingly, it was also emphasised to us that, when leave is refused, the Court is not necessarily saying the Supreme Court should not hear a particular case. Rather, the Court of Appeal's function in this context was said to be the identification of 'that very rare case where ... this jurisdiction needs a result from the Supreme Court pretty quickly'.[24] In other words, by granting leave the Court of Appeal 'is sending a clear message to the final court that the matter is one that needs their urgent attention'.[25] It does not mean 'the final court is more likely to uphold such appeals than those in which permission is granted by the final court itself'.[26]

---

[18] UK Supreme Court, Practice Direction 3, at para 3.3.3.

[19] n 16, para 15.60 and Recommendation CJ134.

[20] Practice Direction 06/2011 (Revised March 2021), available at www.judiciaryni.uk/judicial-decisions/practice-direction-062011-skeleton-arguments-and-related-documents-appeal-books.

[21] See Chapter 8.

[22] J1.

[23] J1, J2, J3, J4, J7.

[24] J1.

[25] Alan Paterson, *Final Judgment: The Last Law Lords and the Supreme Court* (Hart Publishing 2013) 210.

[26] Ibid.

7.4 The number and outcome of appeals

Between the foundation of Northern Ireland on 6 May 1921 and the end of December 2023 there were at least 130 cases from that jurisdiction in which the House of Lords or Supreme Court issued judgments.[27] The vast majority of these cases (113, or 87 per cent) were appeals from the Court of Appeal. A further five were from the Court of Criminal Appeal,[28] although the first of those did not occur until 1961.[29] There were also two appeals to the House of Lords and seven appeals to the Supreme Court from the Divisional Court in Northern Ireland[30] and three references to the Supreme Court by the Attorney General for Northern Ireland.[31] The 118 cases

---

[27] A study of the House of Lords' decision-making in the period 1952 to 1968 reveals that there were 25 unreported decisions (see Louis Blom-Cooper and Gavin Drewry, *Final Appeal: A Study of the House of Lords in its Judicial Capacity* (Clarendon Press 1972) 250–1). Four of these were appeals from Northern Ireland. During other periods – until late 1996, when all decisions began to be published online (see https://publicati ons.parliament.uk/pa/ld/ldjudgmt.htm) – there could have been other unreported decisions in cases brought to the House of Lords from Northern Ireland. If so, they have not been included in the current study.

[28] The Administration of Justice Act 1960 reformed the system for bringing criminal appeals to the Lords from the Court of Appeal in England and Wales or the Court of Appeal in Northern Ireland. It not only required leave to be given either by the Court being appealed against or by the apex court itself. In addition, the Court being appealed against had to certify that a point of law of general public importance was involved. Prior to 1960 appeals in criminal cases in England and Wales could reach the House of Lords only if they were authorised by the fiat of the Attorney General (see Blom-Cooper and Drewry, n 27, 270–5). It seems that no such fiat was ever issued by the Attorney General for Northern Ireland.

[29] *Attorney General for Northern Ireland v Gallagher* [1963] AC 349.

[30] See n 12.

[31] The first of those two references were rejected as premature by the Supreme Court (see [2019] UKSC 1, [2020] NI 793 and [2020] UKSC 2, [2020] NI 820). The third was accepted but the challenge it raised was unsuccessful:

emanating from the Court of Appeal and Court of Criminal Appeal actually involved 131 appeals (including cross-appeals). In the 25-year period from 1999 to 2023 there were 59 cases involving 69 appeals, representing exactly one-half of all appealed cases since 1921.[32] Table 7.2 indicates how many cases were concluded in each decade since the 1920s and how many appeals were allowed (in whole or in part).

As regards the results of the appeals, the overall success rate (43 per cent) is on a par with that for appeals emanating from England and Wales. While the three most recent annual reports of the Supreme Court do not provide detailed figures enabling the success rate of appeals to be calculated with precision, in the previous six financial years (April 2014 to March 2020) the overall success rate was 45 per cent. It is noticeable that in the period 2011 to 2020 the success rate for appeals from Northern Ireland rose to 59 per cent but, given the relatively small numbers of appeals involved and the 30 per cent success rate since 2020, it seems as if the 2010s were an accidental blip and not the harbinger of a trend. Overall, the evidence suggests that the Court of Appeal in Northern Ireland is not operating at an inferior level to that of England and Wales. This assessment contrasts starkly with that made by Blom-Cooper and Drewry in 1972, when they concluded, at least in relation to civil appeals, that

> not only the Northern Irish jurisdiction of the House of Lords is small in size, but also (with a few notable exceptions) trivial in subject-matter. ... It may be that the

---

Reference by the Attorney General for Northern Ireland – Abortion Services (Safe Access Zones) (Northern Ireland) Bill [2022] UKSC 32, [2023] AC 505.

[32] Two Supreme Court cases from Northern Ireland have already been decided in 2024: *Re Hilland's Application* [2024] UKSC 4, on appeal from [2021] NICA 68, and *Re RM's Application* [2004] UKSC 7, on appeal from [2022] NICA 35, [2023] NI 274. Judgment in *Re JR222's Application* [2022] NICA 57 is pending and hearings in four further cases from Northern Ireland are awaited.

judicial process in [a small] country particularly requires the guidance of a senior tribunal, even if this means a few trifling appeals are thereby allowed to reach the House of Lords. Certainly the large percentage of Northern Irish appeals that are successful in the Lords seems to bear this out.[33]

Blom-Cooper and Drewry do not substantiate this conclusion by citing precise figures for the success rate of appeals, but statistics do appear to bear it out. The success rate for appeals from England and Wales in 1952–68 was 35 per cent,[34] while for appeals from Northern Ireland it was 59 per cent. However, since 1968 the success rates for appeals from the two jurisdictions, apart from during the 2010s, have come closer together. It is perhaps the case that in a small jurisdiction there is a greater tendency for judicial 'group-think' and for judges to be more conservative in their approach to novel arguments, but we certainly cannot deduce from that that there is any greater likelihood of professional incompetence.

7.5 The subject matter of appeals

Three of the relatively early appeals from Northern Ireland helped to clarify important aspects of the House of Lords' jurisdiction. First, that it can hear appeals even if they are only about costs;[35] second, that it can deal with any point arising in an appeal even if it is not one on which leave to appeal was

---

[33] Blom-Cooper and Drewry, n 27, 388. This study, at 37, also observed that the presence of Lord MacDermott, a former Lord of Appeal, as Lord Chief Justice in Northern Ireland from 1951 to 1971 weakened the argument that there was a need for strong supervision of the Northern Ireland courts on the part of the House of Lords.

[34] Calculated from the figures at, ibid, 133 (table 7).

[35] *Jennings v Kelly* [1940] AC 206.

Table 7.2: The number of appeals from the Court of Appeal and Court of Criminal Appeal to the House of Lords and Supreme Court, and their outcomes, 1921–2023

	Cases decided	Results of the appeals
1921 to 1930	8	3 appeals allowed 5 appeals dismissed
1931 to 1940	3	0 appeals allowed 3 appeals dismissed
1941 to 1950	4	2 appeals allowed 2 appeals dismissed
1951 to 1960	7[a]	5 appeals allowed 3 appeals dismissed
1961 to 1970	14	6 appeals allowed 8 appeals dismissed
1971 to 1980	6	2 appeals allowed 4 appeals dismissed
1981 to 1990	7[b]	2 appeals allowed 6 appeals dismissed
1991 to 2000	13[c]	4 appeals allowed 11 appeals dismissed
2001 to 2010	24 (HL)[d] 1 (UKSC)	HL: 12 appeals allowed 15 appeals dismissed UKSC: 1 appeal allowed 0 appeals dismissed
2011 to 2020	25[e]	16 appeals allowed 11 appeals dismissed
2021 to 2023	6[f]	3 appeals allowed 7 appeals dismissed
Total	118	56 appeals allowed (43%) 75 appeals dismissed (57%)

[a] In *Scottish Cooperative*, n 58, an appeal was allowed and a cross-appeal was dismissed. [b] There were two appeals in *R v Board of Visitors Maze Prison, ex parte Hone and McCartan* [1988] AC 379. [c] In one case, *Kelly and Loughran v Northern Ireland Housing Executive* [1999] 1 AC 428, the appeal by Ms Kelly was allowed but the appeal by the NIHE in Mr Loughran's case was dismissed. In another case two appeals were conjoined and each was dismissed: *R v Bingham and R v Cooke* [1999] 1 WLR 598. [d] In *Re McClean* [2005] NI 490 the appeal

by the Sentence Review Commissioners was allowed and the cross-appeal by the prisoner was dismissed; in *Jordan v Lord Chancellor*, which was decided alongside *McCaughey v Chief Constable of the Police Service of Northern Ireland* [2007] UKHL 14, [2007] 2 AC 226, the appeal by Mr Jordan was dismissed but the appeal by Mr McCaughey was partly upheld; in *In re D* [2008] UKHL 33, [2008] 1 WLR 1499 the appeal by the Life Sentence Review Commissioners was allowed and the cross-appeal by the prisoner was dismissed. ᵉ In *R (Adams) v Secretary of State for Justice*, n 42 below, the two appeals from Northern Ireland were allowed. In *R v Mackle* [2014] AC 678 there were two appeals, each of which was allowed. ᶠ In *Re Margaret McQuillan's Application* [2021] UKSC 55, [2022] AC 1063, two appeals were allowed and two cross-appeals were dismissed. In *Morgan v Ministry of Justice* [2023] UKSC 14, [2024] AC 130 the Ministry's appeal was allowed and the Public Prosecution Service's cross-appeal was dismissed.

granted;[36] and third, that if there is an even split of opinion among the Lords of Appeal (perhaps because one of the five selected to hear the appeal has died between the hearing and the delivery of judgments) the appeal must be dismissed.[37] By definition these were matters which had not been considered at the Court of Appeal stage in each case. There is nothing to suggest that the current Supreme Court wishes to move away from any of those practices it has inherited from the House of Lords.

More than two fifths of the 118 cases (51, or 43 per cent) involved criminal law, criminal procedure, the powers of the police, or questions concerning inquests. The particular issues dealt with included the defences of drunkenness and automatism,[38] the directions that should be given to a jury when the main evidence against an accused is identificatory or circumstantial,[39] the liability of the army or police for a

---

[36] *Attorney General for Northern Ireland v Gallagher* [1963] AC 349.

[37] *Kennedy v Spratt* [1972] AC 83.

[38] *Gallagher*, n 29, and *Bratty v Attorney General for Northern Ireland* [1963] AC 386 respectively.

[39] *Arthurs v Attorney General for Northern Ireland* (1970) 55 Cr App R 161 and *McGreevy v DPP* [1973] 1 WLR 276 respectively.

death,[40] the admissibility of fresh evidence in an appeal,[41] the definition of a miscarriage of justice,[42] and police powers to stop a protest or parade.[43] As many as 41 cases (35 per cent) were in some way connected with the troubles in Northern Ireland.[44] Altogether, 14 cases involved the police, although the first instance of this was not until 1984.

A further 28 cases (24 per cent) were about other aspects of public law. Eight of these were about rating or taxation issues, but only one has occurred since 1969.[45] On two occasions the legislative powers of the old Northern Ireland Parliament were scrutinised[46] and in recent times the powers of the Northern Ireland Human Rights Commission have twice been examined, including in a case which had significant ramifications for reform of the law on abortion in Northern Ireland.[47]

---

[40] *Attorney-General for Northern Ireland's Reference (No 1 of 1975)* [1977] AC 10; *R v Clegg* [1995] 1 AC 482; *Re McKerr* [2004] UKHL 12, [2004] 1 WLR 807; *Re Geraldine Finucane's Application* [2019] UKSC 7, [2019] 3 All ER 191; *Re Rosaleen Dalton's Application* [2023] UKSC 36, [2023] 3 WLR 671.

[41] *Linton v Ministry of Defence* [1983] NI 51.

[42] *Re McFarland* [2004] 1 WLR 1289 and *R (Adams) v Secretary of State for Justice* [2011] UKSC 18, [2012] 1 AC 48 (which included appeals by two appellants from Northern Ireland).

[43] *E v Chief Constable of the RUC* [2008] UKHL 66, [2009] 1 AC 536 and *DB v Chief Constable of the PSNI* [2017] UKSC 7, [2017] NI 301.

[44] These have been extensively analysed elsewhere: Stephen Livingstone, 'The House of Lords and the Northern Ireland Conflict' (1994) 57 *MLR* 333; Brice Dickson, 'The House of Lords and the Northern Ireland Conflict – A Sequel' (2006) 69 *MLR* 383; Brice Dickson and Conor McCormick, 'Northern Ireland Dimensions to the First Decade of the United Kingdom Supreme Court' (2020) 83 *MLR* 1133.

[45] *IRC v McGuckian* [1997] 1 WLR 991.

[46] *Gallagher v Lynn* [1937] AC 803; *Belfast Corporation v OD Cars Ltd* [1960] AC 490.

[47] *Re NIHRC* [2002] UKHL 25, [2002] NI 236 (overturning the Court of Appeal) and (on abortion) *Re NIHRC's Application* [2018] UKSC 27, [2019] 1 All ER 173 (again, overturning the Court of Appeal). The 2018 decision helped to bring about the decriminalisation of abortion in

Perhaps the public law case with the highest profile is the House of Lords' decision in 2002 (by three votes to two), upholding the majority view in the Court of Appeal, that the election of a First Minister and deputy First Minister outside the six-week period specified in the Northern Ireland Act 1998 was nevertheless valid.[48] In recent times there has been an increase in appeals in judicial review cases (11 between 2014 and 2023).

Finally, another one third of the Northern Ireland cases (39 or 33 per cent) involved private law claims. These were the dominant category of appeals during the first half of the Court of Appeal's existence: 22 of the 35 cases decided before 1970 were private law claims (63 per cent). In the second half they were comparatively rare: 17 out of 83 cases (20 per cent). About a dozen cases have concerned contractual or employment issues,[49] the latter frequently taking the form of claims for injuries at work in the early years and claims for discrimination in the later years.[50] There have been just a handful of cases relating to family law or child law[51] and only two on welfare

---

Northern Ireland through the Northern Ireland (Executive Formation etc) Act 2019, s 9.

[48] *Robinson v Secretary of State for Northern Ireland* [2002] UKHL 32, [2002] NI 390. See Chapter 6.

[49] Contractual cases include *McEvoy v Belfast Banking Co* [1935] AC 24 and *Northern Ireland Hospitals Authority v Whyte* [1963] 1 WLR 882.

[50] For example, *Cavanagh v Ulster Weaving Co Ltd* [1960] AC 145; *Bill v Short Brothers and Harland* [1963] NI 1; *Kelly and Loughran v Northern Ireland Housing Executive* [1999] 1 AC 428; *SCA Packaging Ltd v Boyle* [2009] UKHL 37, [2009] 4 All ER 1181 (see Chapter 4).

[51] For example, *Ward v Laverty* [1925] AC 101; *Down Lisburn Health and Social Service Trust v H* [2006] UKHL 36, [2007] 1 FLR 121 (primarily a public law case); *In re G (Adoption: Unmarried Couple)* [2008] UKHL 38, [2009] 1 AC 173 (also primarily a public law case); *In re K (A Child)* [2014] UKSC 29, [2014] AC 1401; *Makhlouf v Secretary of State for the Home Department* [2016] UKSC 59, [2017] 3 All ER 1 (whether a man's deportation would affect anyone's right to a family life).

law.[52] Possibly the most significant of the few cases on property
or commercial law is a recent one in which the Supreme Court
applied the House of Lords' Practice Statement of 1966 and
departed from a prominent precedent relating to the doctrine
of restraint of trade.[53] The Court of Appeal, of course, had
felt bound by that precedent.[54]

7.6 Appeals against judgments of Chief Justices

It is interesting to consider the record of the ten Chief Justices
of Northern Ireland – who are *ex officio* Presidents of the Court
of Appeal – regarding appeals taken against their judgments in
the Court of Appeal to the House of Lords or the Supreme
Court. Table 7.3 summarises the figures.

A recurring feature in the appeals heard in the 1950s
and 1960s was the deference paid by the Law Lords to the
judgments of Lord MacDermott CJ in cases from Northern
Ireland. In two cases his view as the trial judge was preferred
to that of the Court of Appeal,[55] in one case his concurring
judgment in the Court of Appeal was upheld[56] and in three
cases his dissenting judgments in the Court of Appeal were
approved.[57] On the other hand, on five occasions his views as

---

[52] *Kerr v Department for Social Development* [2004] UKHL 23, [2004] 1 WLR
1372; *Re McLaughlin's Application* [2018] UKSC 48, [2018] 1 WLR 4250.

[53] *Peninsula Securities Ltd v Dunnes Stores (Bangor) Ltd* [2020] UKSC 36,
[2021] AC 1014, departing from *Esso Petroleum Co Ltd v Harper's Garage
(Stourport) Ltd* [1968] AC 269.

[54] [2018] NICA 7; interestingly, the trial judge, McBride J, had not felt so
constrained: she stressed that none of the Law Lords in the *Esso Petroleum*
case had stated that the restraint of trade doctrine should extend to
successors in title of the original covenantor.

[55] *Gallagher*, n 29; *Northern Ireland Hospitals Authority v Whyte* [1963] 1
WLR 882.

[56] *IRC v Herdman* [1969] 1 WLR 1919.

[57] *Cavanagh*, n 50; *Bill*, n 50; *Irwin v White, Tomkins and Courage* [1964] 1
WLR 387.

Table 7.3: Appeals against judgments of the Chief Justices, 1921–2023

Name and period of service	Number of judgments appealed	Number and percentage of judgments reversed*
Sir Denis Henry 1921–25	1	1 (100%)
Sir William Moore 1925–37	4	2 (50%)
Sir James Andrews 1937–51	5	3 (60%)
Lord MacDermott 1951–71	15	5 (33%)
Sir Robert Lowry 1971–88	7	2 (29%)
Sir Brian Hutton 1988–97	8	2 (25%)
Sir Robert Carswell 1997–2004	11	6 (55%)
Sir Brian Kerr 2004–09	9	7 (78%)
Sir Declan Morgan 2009–21	17	12 (71%)
Dame Siobhan Keegan 2021–	1	0 (0%)

* 'Reversed' refers here to judgments of the LCJ with which the House of Lords disagreed, including dissenting judgments.

a Court of Appeal judge were not wholly endorsed.[58] Lord MacDermott's expertise was well known to the House because in 1947, having served for just three years as a High Court judge in Northern Ireland, he was whisked to London to serve as a Lord of Appeal. His more senior colleagues in Belfast who were overlooked for the role included the then Lord Chief Justice, Sir James Andrews.[59] On the death of Sir James in 1951

---

[58] *McClelland v Northern Ireland General Health Services Board* [1957] 1 WLR 594; *Smyth v Cameron* (1959, unreported); *Scottish Cooperative Wholesale Society Ltd v Ulster Farmers' Mart Co Ltd* [1960] AC 63; *OD Cars*, n 46; *McEldowney v Forde* [1971] AC 632.

[59] According to the Dictionary of Irish Biography (available at www.dib.ie), Andrews was appointed as LCJ only because his brother John, who was a

Lord MacDermott returned to Northern Ireland to take up the position of Lord Chief Justice, a role he retained for the following 20 years. During that time he sat as an *ad hoc* Law Lord on more than 25 occasions,[60] although never in an appeal from Northern Ireland.

Lord MacDermott's successor as Lord Chief Justice was Sir Robert Lowry. He too never sat in a Northern Irish appeal in the House of Lords, either as an *ad hoc* judge before 1988 or as a full-time Lord of Appeal from 1988 to 1994. Sir Brian Hutton succeeded Lord Lowry as Lord Chief Justice of Northern Ireland in 1988 and then as a Lord of Appeal in 1997. It was only in 2001 that he became the first former judge from Northern Ireland to hear an appeal from the Court of Appeal in that jurisdiction[61] and he went on to hear a further five. Lord Hutton's successor both as Lord Chief Justice and as Lord of Appeal, Lord Carswell, heard 11 cases from Northern Ireland and in turn Lord Kerr, who followed Lord Carswell in the same two roles, heard no fewer than 22.[62] Since Lord Kerr's replacement by Lord Stephens as a Supreme Court Justice the latter has heard four appeals from Northern Ireland while the retired Lord Chief Justice, Sir Declan Morgan, has

---

minister in the government of Northern Ireland at the time, insisted upon it. Lord Craigavon, the then Prime Minister, had allegedly promised the role to the serving Attorney General, Sir Anthony Babington. Instead Babington took up the vacancy on the Court of Appeal created by Andrews's promotion.

[60] According to Blom-Cooper and Drewry, n 27, 176, that is the number of his appearances between 1952 and 1968. He sat in a further nine cases in the House of Lords before retiring from his *ad hoc* role in 1973.

[61] This was in *McGrath v Chief Constable of the RUC* [2001] 2 AC 731.

[62] We have analysed elsewhere Lord Kerr's record regarding appeals to the House of Lords against his own judgments in Northern Ireland: Brice Dickson and Conor McCormick, 'The Development of Lord Kerr's Judicial Mind' in Brice Dickson and Conor McCormick (eds), *The Judicial Mind: A Festschrift for Lord Kerr of Tonaghmore* (Hart Publishing 2021) 8–12.

heard one such appeal as an *ad hoc* judge and his successor, Lady Chief Justice Keegan, has heard two.[63] In our interviews with a range of Court of Appeal judges, we learned that one felt it was prudent for a Lord or Lady Chief Justice, whether retired or in office, to sit on the Supreme Court from time to time in order to avoid the 'danger' of over-reliance on the influential views of the permanent Supreme Court judge from Northern Ireland.[64] However, it was acknowledged that such opportunities would be limited, given that the Chief Justice is normally involved in the high-profile cases that are decided by the Court of Appeal.[65]

We should not read too much into the 'reversal rate' for Chief Justices' judgments in the Court of Appeal that are appealed to a higher court. So much depends on whether the Chief Justice felt bound by a precedent, whether the arguments put in the Court of Appeal were different from those put in the House of Lords or Supreme Court and whether the case was one which required a novel solution that it was more appropriate for a final appeal court to adopt than an intermediate one. It is, however, clear that during the past 25 years there has been a marked increase in the success rate for appeals taken against judgments of the Chief Justices. This may betoken a failure on the part of counsel to put their arguments across in a convincing enough manner in the Court of Appeal or perhaps a relative timidity on the part of the Chief Justices to accept their arguments. We cannot point to any common feature in recent appeals that suggests that Chief Justices are in any way falling down on the job. A likely explanation for the rise in the success rate of appeals is the growing complexity of the law and the correlative scope that exists for reasonable disagreements to emerge over finer points. As one of our

---

[63] The Lady Chief Justice also sat in one case that was *referred* to the Supreme Court: *Abortion Services (Safe Access Zones)*, n 31.

[64] J1.

[65] J7.

judicial interviewees put it, 'there is not really a right answer in the sense that a court at different times could decide either way in most cases, or decide differently in most cases depending on the composition of the court'.[66] It also seems that both Lord Carswell and Lord Kerr became more 'activist' judges once they moved from being the head of a small devolved jurisdiction to serving as one of a group of judges at the apex of the national court system.

7.7 Conclusion

In our interviews with the judges, one said: 'When you are sitting in the Court of Appeal, you are conscious of the fact that you could go to the Supreme Court. ... You do not just have the freedom to do whatever you like. You have got to justify it.'[67]

Similar sentiments have been captured by previous research involving members of the Court of Appeal in England and Wales, with one of them having said 'you are writing defensively to a certain extent to armour plate yourself against appeal'.[68] This much confirms, unsurprisingly, that members of both courts are alive to the possibility of being held judicially accountable for the rigour of their judgments.

This chapter has also confirmed that judgments by top judges in Northern Ireland are not always endorsed by their 'superiors' in London, but that their record in that respect is no worse than that of judges sitting in the Court of Appeal in England and Wales. In most cases in which London-based judges have disagreed with Belfast-based ones, it is not because the latter have been deemed to have made mistakes in their application of the law but rather because the former have decided to clarify

---

[66] J6.

[67] J4.

[68] Paterson, n 25, 210. For Paterson's analysis of the rather more 'fraught' relationship between the final court of appeal and the Scots, see 233–46.

the law in ways that could not have been confidently predicted by the lower court. While the Supreme Court is keen to avoid undesirable differences arising between how similar laws are applied in various jurisdictions within the UK,[69] it also appears to recognise the value of entering into a written 'dialogue' with senior judges in the intermediate appeal courts below it.[70]

---

[69] For example, *Re RM's Application*, n 32.

[70] Paterson, n 25, 209–13; Alan Paterson, *The Law Lords* (Macmillan Press 1982) 85–7.

EIGHT

Conservation and
Reform Reflections

8.1 Introduction

A plethora of interesting revelations emerged from our
interviews with a range of judges who have served on
the Court of Appeal in Northern Ireland.[1] By peppering
quotations from those interviews throughout the preceding
chapters of this book, we have sought to share relevant
judicial viewpoints in the context of our historical, statistical,
and qualitative case law analyses wherever possible. In this
chapter we intend to concentrate on our conversations with
the judges in their own right. We will examine their views
on three groups of issues in particular, highlighting policy
areas where there seems to exist a consensus in favour of
either conservation or reform, in addition to policy areas
where the judges' views are mixed. First, we will explore
some judicial opinions on whether the legislative framework
that governs the Court of Appeal should be changed in
any way. Second, we will consider whether the judges we
have spoken to believe there are any procedural or practical
aspects of the way the Court of Appeal works that could be
usefully reformed without the need for legislation. Finally,
we will unpack some judicial reflections about the role of
the President of the Court of Appeal.

---

[1] See Chapter 1 for details of our methodology.

At a granular level, we trust that our analysis of various comments and proposals shared by the judges will be a useful starting point for policy development by those who are formally responsible for it at some point in the future. We hope, at least, to provide a helpful window into senior judicial thinking about what works well and what progress might entail. At a more macro level, we believe our interview analysis advances one of the academic aims of this book in so far as it sheds light on what Northern Ireland appellate judges do and think beyond the pages of their judgments. In particular, we will highlight the extent to which our interviewees revealed a fairly consistent propensity to balance pragmatism with idealism when considering each of the discussion points we explored with them. Far from being inherently conservative, in the non-political sense of the word, our conversations with the judges suggest that they are largely open-minded to evidence-based changes to their governance and indeed eager to pilot new initiatives.

8.2 The legislative framework for the Court

Some of the previous chapters in this book have explained the historical development of the statutory framework for the Court of Appeal, culminating most notably in the Judicature (NI) Act 1978,[2] as well as the statutes which currently confer jurisdiction on the Court by creating specific rights of appeal from various lower courts and tribunals.[3] Interestingly, when we asked our interviewees for their views on this legislative scheme, we received an assortment of responses on whether an essentially comprehensive review was required. On the one hand, we heard from a judge who was unaware of any problems with the present statutory framework[4] and another

---

[2]   See Chapter 2.
[3]   See Chapters 4–5.
[4]   J3.

who said 'it works satisfactorily in practice' and has 'not been found wanting'.[5] On the other hand, we spoke to a judge who thought that while the 1978 Act, in particular, 'achieves its purpose', it was 'out of date' and needed reform in order to 'catch up'.[6] Similarly, another judge told us that 'an Access to Justice Act of some sort is ... an important bit of structural work that needs to be done here'.[7] Falling somewhere between these two poles, a different judge shared the following comments:

> If there was a functioning Law Commission, political will and funding, I am quite sure people would enthusiastically look again at some of our procedures. But we shrug our shoulders and say, well, we don't have an Assembly. The rules are really hard to change. We have to do stuff by Practice Direction, and there is no way you are going to get an amendment. ... There is just an assumption that these things are not worth the candle at the moment.[8]

As our conversations with all of the judges unfolded, however, it became clear that even those who did not favour wholesale reform of the statutory framework, and those who were apathetic, were nonetheless keen to explore discrete changes in response to particular challenges. There were three statutory areas in particular that came up for discussion in most of our interviews: namely, the rules on leave to appeal; the scope of appeal rights, particularly in cases involving the judicial review of a criminal cause or matter; and the size of the bench, both as limited overall and as limited in particular cases. In the following sub-sections, we will consider the judges' reflections on each

---

[5] J5.
[6] J7.
[7] J1.
[8] J2. There was no functioning Assembly when this interview took place, but it has since been restored.

of these areas in turn before summarising some miscellaneous reflections about the statutory framework thereafter.

8.2.1 The rules on leave to appeal

A reasonably strong majority of our interviewees was in favour of uniformly requiring leave to appeal to the Court of Appeal in civil cases, as it already is in criminal cases, though some were more certain about the need for this than others. From a practical point of view, one judge regarded the idea with some ambivalence given that the Court is generally able to process civil appeals quite quickly under present arrangements:

> I think the question is whether in this jurisdiction you would be making more or less work for yourself. If you look at the ability to get a civil case in the Court of Appeal: you will generally be offered a slot within three [or] four working months, something in that order, to deal with the case. It might be reviewed once in the course of that if it was thought necessary. I can understand why it is absolutely critical in jurisdictions where they have got limited slots to deal with the cases that they have got. I do not think it is urgent here. I have no objection to it, but I do not think it is urgent.[9]

Similarly, another judge weighed up the considerations in these terms:

> The jury really is out on this. ... I think, first of all, it would mean lots more work for the puisne judges doing leave decisions. ... Maybe that's not a reason itself not to have it, but that would be a practical reality. Then the second thing is I think inevitably you would have to

---

[9] J1.

offer litigants a chance to review the application orally before the court in any event. Query whether you would really be saving very much in terms of time and resource by creating another layer. Yes, you might be able to knock out the totally hopeless reasonably quickly, but I am not sure whether it would be particularly effective if the threshold was just arguability. I suspect a lot of applications would be granted and therefore query whether it would make a lot of difference to the running of our courts. We have all seen cases that are just rubbish and we would say to ourselves: that should have really never got to the Court of Appeal. But it is still a relatively small number, I think. I wax and wane, in that I am not convinced either way at the minute.[10]

Likewise, we heard the practicality of the reform proposal framed and considered as follows:

One would have to work out what the mechanics would be. The critical question for the model would be whether a decision of a Court of Appeal judge or a panel of Court of Appeal judges refusing leave to appeal would be final or capable of being renewed, which is the English system. We would have to draw on their experience and their statistics in order to determine whether this might simply incur a greater investment of judicial resource and greater delays with no particular gain.[11]

Other judges were 'strongly of the view there should be some filter system',[12] with the challenges presented by a rise in the presence of litigants in person being a frequently cited

---

[10] J2.
[11] J5.
[12] J4.

justification for it.[13] While one judge expressed reservations about whether it was 'a very good principled reason' to introduce a leave stage simply in order 'to deny personal litigants another bite of the cherry',[14] another did in fact articulate their support for the proposal in substantially principled terms:

> I think there has to be some filter, and that is not just for the convenience of the court. That is to save public money, and I think to properly not give people the expectation that you can bring an appeal which is not formulated at all or is meaningless. That you just have a right to argue a case. ... In other words, it is not coming from a place that is trying to restrict appeals. It is simply trying to streamline appeals.[15]

8.2.2 The scope of certain appeal rights

Two discrete issues arising from our conversations about the present scope of appeal rights are notable at this stage.

The first concerns the current rights of appeal in respect of judicial reviews involving a criminal cause or matter which, as we have explained elsewhere,[16] must be decided by a Divisional Court at first instance and cannot be appealed by the applicant to the Court of Appeal thereafter – an appeal to the Supreme Court lies only at the instance of the defendant or prosecutor, assuming the restrictive test for permission to that Court is met. There was an essentially unanimous view among the judges whom we spoke to about this issue,[17] in

---

[13] J2; J3; J4; J5; J6.

[14] J2.

[15] J7.

[16] See Chapter 5.

[17] With the exception of J3, who said it was not something they had a strong view about.

favour of reform, though we detected some divergences in opinion as regards the basis of their desire for change and the best model with which to replace the present rules. Several judges pointed to the difficulties they have experienced when called upon to interpret the phrase 'criminal cause or matter' as it appears in the Judicature (NI) Act 1978. Notwithstanding some ostensible clarification provided by the Supreme Court in *Re McGuinness's Application*,[18] our Court of Appeal judges maintain that 'it still throws up interpretative issues which distract the Court and take a lot of time to resolve'.[19] Indeed the time taken up by such interpretative issues was noted by several judges,[20] with one saying 'you have nonsensical situations where two judges are sitting hearing a leave application just in case it's a criminal cause of matter, which is a total waste of resources'.[21] In addition, some judges stressed that 'arguably, the point is that people lose a strong appellate right if they are captured by criminal cause or matter'.[22] One elaborated on the serious nature of the problem in this way:

> [It] has created this unfair appeal structure where in some cases litigants only have one bite of the cherry, whereas in other cases that are not particularly different you have got three, and that seems to me to be farcical. If, as we do, we treat the decisions of the PPS whether or not to prosecute, as criminal causes or matters ... and therefore heard by a Divisional Court, you have a situation there where the PPS, if aggrieved, has a right at least to seek an appeal to the Supreme Court, but the family of

---

18 [2020] UKSC 6, [2021] AC 392.
19 J7.
20 J2; J5; J6; J7.
21 J2.
22 J7; J2.

the victim has no appeal right whatsoever, and that is just nonsensical.[23]

When discussing the best model to replace the current rules, a range of ideas was suggested to us. One judge felt so strongly about the need to avoid unnecessary duplication that they proposed 'there should be a kind of leapfrog right for every case' which would involve identifying cases at first instance that are likely to require the attention of the Supreme Court and providing a direct appeal route to that Court in order to avoid the production of multiple judgments in several of the courts below.[24] Another said:

> You could widen section 41[25] to allow an appeal from the Divisional Court by anybody to the Supreme Court, with the same hurdles of certification of a question. That is one way to solve it. The cleaner way is to do away with the distinction altogether, have everything heard by a High Court Judge sitting alone, first instance in judicial review, with the same appeal rights that everybody else has. That seems to me to be just a much more straightforward application of both principle and practice.[26]

However, when asked to reflect on the second proposal outlined in the previous quotation, one of the judges warned that care should be taken to 'place some filter on appeals to the Supreme Court in criminal law on a point of law because of the nature of criminal cases: the need for certainty'.[27]

The second discrete issue arising from our conversations about the present scope of appeal rights concerns whether it

---

[23] J2.
[24] J6.
[25] Judicature (NI) Act 1978.
[26] J2.
[27] J7.

should be possible to appeal cases all the way to the Supreme Court regardless of where they start out. One of the judges referred to the fact that in civil appeals by way of case stated from the county court to the Court of Appeal, for example, the Court of Appeal's judgment is statutorily final unless a devolution issue has arisen, as in the conspicuous case of *Lee v Ashers Baking Company Ltd*.[28] The judge thought it was 'wrong as a matter of principle' that that case was only able to reach the Supreme Court 'by the most circuitous of routes' when it was widely regarded as 'an important case' and could not be appealed in the normal way simply because it had commenced in the county court.[29] Other judges had sympathy with this view,[30] but regarded the scenario as 'one in a million'.[31] Moreover, several interviewees felt it was important to emphasise that 'there is nothing wrong in principle with the Northern Ireland Court of Appeal being the final Court of Appeal for certain types of case'.[32]

8.2.3 The size of the bench

There are three notable issues to record from our conversations with the judges as regards the size of the Court of Appeal.

---

[28] J2; [2018] UKSC 49, [2019] 1 All ER 1. See Chapter 6.

[29] J2.

[30] J1; J7.

[31] J1. J2, however, referred to the case of *Brady v Northern Ireland Housing Executive* [1990] NI 200 as an example of a case which could not be appealed beyond the Court of Appeal, meaning another case had to be 'manufactured' in order to get the relevant point of law before the House of Lords, namely, *McGeown v Northern Ireland Housing Executive* [1995] 1 AC 233. The question at issue was whether a person using a public right of way did so by right and could not therefore be the 'visitor' of the owner of the land for the purposes of the Occupiers' Liability Act (NI) 1957.

[32] J5; J7.

The first issue concerns a statutory limitation on the number of judges who can be designated to sit in an appeal. The maximum number of judges who can hear any particular matter arising in the Court of Appeal is capped at three.[33] One of the judges we spoke to indicated that in a difficult case it might be helpful if the Court was empowered to sit as a panel of five 'in order to make clear where the law stands'.[34] They did not regard this as a 'critical issue', but thought it was worth sharing the idea for consideration, not least because the Court of Appeal in England and Wales does not face the same statutory constraint and has in fact sat as a panel of five in order to modify earlier lines of case law.[35] Likewise, the Supreme Court has published criteria governing when it will sit as a panel of more than five Justices and has done so in several high-profile cases.[36] The judge we spoke to suggested that 'the four members of the Court of Appeal and the senior High Court judge' could be enlisted to establish a particularly authoritative precedent, if the relevant statutory provision was amended to enable an enlarged court formation in appropriate cases.[37]

The second notable issue as regards the size of the Court of Appeal concerns a statistical increase in the use of two-person panels over the course of the past several years.[38] When we asked our interviewees about the rationale for having two-person panels, we gleaned a number of helpful insights. One said:

---

[33] Judicature (NI) Act 1978, s 36.

[34] J1.

[35] J1. See, for example, *R v F(S)* [2011] EWCA Crim 1844, [2012] QB 703 (Lord Judge CJ, Hughes and Goldring LJJ, Ouseley and Dobbs JJ).

[36] See 'Panel numbers criteria' on the UK Supreme Court website, available at www.supremecourt.uk/procedures/panel-numbers-criteria.html. Also see Robert Reed, 'Collective Judging in the UK Supreme Court' in Birke Häcker and Wolfgang Ernst (eds), *Collective Judging in Comparative Perspective: Counting Votes and Weighing Opinions* (Intersentia 2020) 27.

[37] J1.

[38] See Chapter 3 for details of our statistical analysis on this point.

Sometimes it is a convenience thing, and you would not see this in cases that ... are obviously of great moment and need three ... sometimes they are coming from the magistrates' court; they are important issues, but they are not at the apex, so they would have twos quite a bit. The simple reason for it, I think, is to do with the subject matter. If the two disagree, you have to hear it again with another person, but that very rarely happens, because, as I said, these are not identified as the most difficult or challenging cases.[39]

Another judge said:

The first question I think that raises is has that given rise to a difficulty? I am pretty certain that it resulted in a disagreement in only one case in the last number of years, and that appeal was then transferred to a new panel of three judges for a hearing afresh. Interestingly enough that particular problem has not arisen. The second question is a very interesting one and that is whether the public and the professions should be aware of the criteria for selecting a panel of two. I am not aware of any outcry in favour of that. I suppose on balance I would favour leaving the Chief Justice with a broad discretion in the matter of selection of panels and the number of panel members.[40]

Nonetheless, the same judge informed us:

Much of the routine business of the Court of Appeal can be very efficiently and properly transacted by a panel that does not have to consist of three of the four senior

---

[39] J7.
[40] J5.

THE COURT OF APPEAL IN NORTHERN IRELAND

judges, but approximately one third ... is better dealt
with by a panel of three from the four because of the
complexity, importance, public perception, expectations
of the parties and the public. I do believe that those are the
criteria which should normally shape the composition
of the panel.[41]

The risk of a stalemate in the event of disagreement between
two judges, which would require a re-hearing with three,[42]
was also raised by other judges.[43] As one of them put it:

There is a difficulty because you do not want to say that
you have decided the case in advance, but if you have
only got two judges, you have got to have unanimity.
You have three in case there is not. If you are going in
with two, then you may have to reconvene with three if
you find there is disagreement.[44]

With these reasons in mind, a fair proportion of the judges
we spoke to seemed to have 'a strong preference'[45] for three-
person panels. One said they simply 'work better',[46] while
another said they were aware of 'feedback' from people who
were 'not happy' about the use of two-person panels because
'they felt the appeals were not being taken as seriously as they
should'.[47] This led one of the judges to say that there should
be 'three person courts for virtually everything'.[48] There is
therefore still room for debate regarding whether the statutory

---

[41] J5.
[42] Judicature (NI) Act 1978, s 36(3).
[43] J2; J4; J6.
[44] J6.
[45] J2.
[46] J4.
[47] J1.
[48] J1.

power of the Chief Justice to convene two-person panels should be altered.

Interestingly, when we asked our interviewees whether the recent increase in two-person panels had been necessitated by a shortage in judicial resources, we were told that this was not the case. This was because all of the judges we spoke to regarded their 'High Court colleagues as able substitutes for the Court of Appeal',[49] and because the Chief Justice is also able to draw on the support of retired Lords Justices if necessary.

As regards the use of puisne judges, all of our interviewees were quite strongly of the view that this was a positive practice. One judge described it as 'essential' because sitting on the Court of Appeal substantially enhances a High Court judge's understanding of how their own decisions might be scrutinised on appeal.[50] Another judge emphasised that High Court judges play an important role in certain Court of Appeal cases primarily because they 'bring expertise, particularly in the area of crime'.[51] A different judge justified the practice predominantly by reference to the 'training aspect' of the opportunity it provides to puisne judges, and because it 'was always going to improve collegiality'.[52] By way of a small reservation, we were advised that while there was no harm in having one or even two puisne judges sitting on a Court of Appeal case, some care should be taken to avoid the possibility or perception of undue deference from one to the other, which could arise, for example, if the Lord or Lady Chief Justice was to sit on a two-person panel with a very junior High Court judge.[53] In contrast, another judge observed that 'you might get an equally forceful puisne judge and others who are more

---

[49] J1.
[50] J6. J1 expressed a similar view.
[51] J7.
[52] J1.
[53] J3.

consensus driven', adding that 'that is just the way lawyers divide up in any walk of life'.[54]

As regards retired judges, we were informed that they have been drawn upon to populate Court of Appeal panels over recent years either because they were involved in particular cases prior to retirement that the Chief Justice asked them to finish,[55] or in order to 'fill gaps'.[56] One of our interviewees elaborated in this way:

> Their use has been driven by necessity, by and large. The necessity is on a very genuine basis. One, the lack of manpower, which really was the main reason for drawing on retired judges, but very occasionally, there were cases where the number of judges available for other reasons to form a panel was extremely small, i.e. judges who could not, for recusal-type reasons, form a panel. If it can be avoided, a Court of Appeal panel should not consist of retired judges only. ... I think everybody would probably agree with that. Secondly, it is better for a Court of Appeal panel to have at least two serving judges. That is another principle which I would put forward.[57]

As the start of that quotation illustrates, some judges acknowledged that there was a resourcing issue for at least some of the 25-year period focused on in this book. We understand that the issue stemmed from a shortfall in the High Court complement over a number of years, which reduced the pool of puisne judges from which the Court of Appeal could draw. Notwithstanding these events, quite a number of the judges we spoke to were doubtful when we suggested that perhaps a

---

[54] J2.
[55] J1.
[56] J7.
[57] J5.

fourth Lord or Lady Justice of Appeal may be required.[58] The various mechanisms for dispatching the workload of the Court that we have adumbrated earlier – the ability of the Chief Justice to convene two-person panels together with the availability of puisne and retired judges – led several judges to doubt whether such an appointment was necessary.[59] However, two of the judges we spoke to suggested some persuasive reasons in favour of expanding the Court.[60] Significantly, it was put to us that 'there certainly would be enough work in the appellate court' to justify a fourth position.[61] In addition, those in favour of expansion adverted to the fact that the number of judges on the High Court has expanded significantly over the years,[62] whereas the number of Lords/Ladies Justices has expanded only once, in 1975, from two to three. This, we heard, might be viewed as having created a 'slightly unbalanced' distribution of senior judges:

> You do not want to have a Court of Appeal that has no Lords Justices. You probably do not want to have it all that often [that] you have only got one. If you have two plus a puisne, that seems to me to be fine. Maybe that balance would be easier struck if you have the Chief and four LJs.[63]

Lastly, as against the argument that to expand the Court of Appeal might reduce the frequency with which puisne judges would be offered the opportunity to gain experience at that level, one of our interviewees pointed out that while that was true, 'there would be more natural progression for High Court

---

58 For the statistical analysis which led to us to this proposal, see Chapter 3.
59 J1, J5, J6.
60 J2, J7.
61 J7. J2 held a similar view.
62 See Chapter 2.
63 J2.

judges to get to the Court of Appeal if there were four rather than three',[64] in the sense that there would be more appellate court posts to apply for in the long run.

8.2.4 Other statutory suggestions

Before turning to the non-statutory issues explored in our conversations with the judges, there are two issues which *would* require statutory amendments that can be noted in relatively brief terms here. The first is that one of our interviewees suggested it might be helpful to confer an express power on the Court of Appeal to refer relevant parties to mediation or arbitration in appropriate cases.[65] In the public law context, for instance, our interviewee wondered 'whether sometimes encouraging mediation as a resolution to some of these issues might produce a better outcome than simply going through the courts'.[66] The second issue was suggested to us by a different judge who indicated that the present Lady Chief Justice was planning to evaluate the possibility of broadcasting sentencing remarks made in the Court of Appeal by way of a 'not-for-broadcast pilot'.[67] If the Chief Justice was minded to proceed with that initiative beyond the pilot, legislation would be needed to remove the statutory prohibition of any filming with a view to publication. This prompted our interviewee to reflect on the regrettable fact that while there was clearly 'good will to do things' within the Court of Appeal, 'getting them copper fastened' was stymied by the lack of a working Executive at the time of our interview.

---

[64] J7.
[65] J1.
[66] J2.
[67] J7.

8.3 The administrative functioning of the Court

Several of the issues that have been surveyed through the prism of statutory conservation and reform as outlined in the previous section could also have been analysed from a more administrative point of view. Having registered that caveat to our chosen structure for this chapter, we now wish to document some matters which have not been mentioned thus far because they involve conservation and reform ideas which are more clearly non-statutory in nature.

We have been told that there is an issue of non-compliance with the Court of Appeal Practice Direction and with case management direction orders more generally.[68] One judge summarised the associated administrative problems like this:

There is a daily problem in the Court of Appeal which arises out of a cultural difficulty prevailing in the legal profession, and that is repeated non-compliance with Practice Directions and specific case management directions. I would love everyone to get around the table to try to address that issue. We have done our best in the Court of Appeal, but it gives rise to a disproportionate investment of judicial resources. Judges should really be preparing for hearings, dealing with hearings, and writing judgments, that is what the circle should entail all the time. I do not object at all to case management. In fact, I am big in favour of it and I always have been, but we

---

[68] See Practice Direction 06/2011 (Revised March 2021), available at www.judiciaryni.uk/judicial-decisions/practice-direction-062011-skele ton-arguments-and-related-documents-appeal-books. Also see FORM COAC1 [REV 1 March 2021], available at the same link. Lastly, see Interim Practice Direction 01/2020 [REV 2] in respect of remote hearings before the Court of Appeal, available at www.judiciaryni.uk/ judicial-decisions/interim-practice-direction-01-2020-rev-2-remote-hearings.

have to invest too much resource because of the default of the profession.[69]

In practical terms, the same judge explained that this problem tended to manifest itself in two ways. The 'main problem' is non-compliance with time limits and a failure to provide 'hearing bundles, authority bundles, electronic bundles, that sort of thing' in accordance with the relevant guidelines.[70] The other problem is that 'the content is of variable quality'.[71] Particularising, our interviewee said:

> The judge will be focusing ... [*inter alia*] ... on the formulation of the grounds of appeal. If there is any lack of coherence or repetition, or if there are simply far too many, then one of the main aims of case management from that point will be to achieve narrow, focused grounds. Coherence. In every case, that is a very desirable objective. In every case, it is achievable. It is the judge taking the lead, the judge being proactive, investment of judicial resource, and so forth. That is cultural also. One would hope that that culture can be improved.[72]

This sentiment was echoed by another judge who agreed that the grounds of appeal initially articulated by counsel certainly tended to be 'much too generalised' at one point in time.[73] However, multiple judges acknowledged that there has been improvement in these areas over more recent times. One said:

> We have got a pretty rigorous Practice Direction, which is not always adhered to, but most of the cases are

---

[69] J5.
[70] J5.
[71] J5.
[72] J5.
[73] J6.

reasonably well case managed, it seems to me. Some of them very well case managed, depending on who is in charge. I think, to be fair, when you get to the actual hearing most cases are pretty well defined and prepared. The points at issue are isolated and dealt with and that means, in my experience, the oral hearings are actually quite short because the parties have been put to their mettle on what points are actually of substance here and what needs to be pursued through case management.[74]

Allied to this issue, we were informed of cultural challenges that the Court of Appeal has also encountered in the context of its efforts to advance a programme of digitalisation.[75] For instance, although the Lady Chief Justice has provided that 'all authorities should be digital', one of our interviewees estimated that this rule was observed by lawyers and by the judges themselves only about 50 per cent of the time in practice.[76]

8.4 The role of the President

There is an overlap between the previous section and this one in so far as the President of the Court of Appeal – that is, the Lord or Lady Chief Justice – could be regarded as playing a largely administrative role. However, following our conversations with the judges we believe we can confirm that the managerial influence of the role tends to bleed into jurisprudential leadership in certain respects as well.

The role comes with at least three important powers that can substantively influence the work of the Court of Appeal. The first is the President's responsibility for allocating cases to particular panels of judges. Revealingly, one of the

---

[74] J2.
[75] J7. See www.judiciaryni.uk/digital-modernisation.
[76] J7.

judges we spoke to recalled the following interaction with a former President:

> He actually said to me once, 'It is a very important power of the Chief Justice to be able to pick the other members of the court'. I do not want to invent the next sentence or two after that, but it was not just about their abilities and expertise. He meant to get the right results.[77]

As an illustration of the outworkings of this approach, the same judge told us that they had not been provided with 'the opportunity to be in that many heavy cases, partly because of time and partly because ... of this judge selection thing'.[78] A different judge shared similar reflections when they hypothesised that 'if you are on a whole load of uninteresting cases, you might suspect that you have done something to annoy [the President]'.[79] At the same time, we were told that judicial workloads are 'fairly divided'[80] and that the specialist expertise of particular judges appears to be the most commonly used criterion for allocations.[81] Our sense was that most of the judges we spoke to felt the President is entitled to retain the broad discretion they currently have in respect of panel choices.

The second important decision-making power of the President relates to the designation of lead judgment writers. We learned from our interviews that the President of the Court 'stars' the name of one of the judges selected to sit on a case,[82] which indicates that they will be writing the lead judgment:

---

[77] J3.

[78] J3.

[79] J4.

[80] J4.

[81] J2.

[82] 'Starring' is the term most interviewees used to describe the process of assigning judgment writers.

What happens is that there is an asterisk put against your name and you know that you are the judgment writer. ... You undoubtedly do look at the case differently if you are the judgment writer. It is up to you then to tap your colleagues, to find out what they think and get their views on any points, and then try and reach, through argument, an agreement as to what you think the right result should be.[83]

While we understand that this has been the default approach for the last ten years or so,[84] we were also informed that the assignment of lead judgment writing work at such an early stage 'is not set in stone' and that the responsibility for lead judgment writing is occasionally re-allocated.[85] Several judges seemed reasonably content with this early assignment model, but we did receive representations from some who intimated that it was sub-optimal. The two downsides noted to us were, first, that early assignments 'might discourage other members of the court from taking as close an interest in the case as they might otherwise'[86] and, second, that 'there is too much focus on one judge and one judgment'.[87] Expanding on the second point, one interviewee explained that while assigning lead judgment writers early has not given rise to controversy, 'it does discourage dissenting judgments' in the sense that 'a panel of three can come to an agreement among a majority of two and a third member who has differing views' because 'the third member is not all that likely to write a dissenting judgment'.[88] This was 'not desirable' because, as the judge put

---

[83] J4.
[84] J6.
[85] J5.
[86] J1.
[87] J5.
[88] J5.

it, 'dissenting judgments may be tomorrow's law'.[89] Other judges also recognised that there is value in having a culture whereby dissents are not actively discouraged,[90] though there seems to be a consensus around the idea that the present Court of Appeal enjoys 'a good collegiate atmosphere' whereby individual members of the Court are able to argue amicably over the issues until a consensus is reached in most cases.[91]

The third notable power of the President concerns their influence as the presiding judge in cases in which they sit. We were interested to discover that, in addition to sitting on 'high-profile'[92] cases because of the importance of the issues at stake and the perceived 'clout' of issuing a judgment from the Chief Justice in those contexts,[93] there has evolved 'an unspoken rule that the Chief Justice should take the lead, and be seen to take the lead, in the most important criminal appeals against conviction and appeals against sentence'.[94] It was explained to us that, while this practice 'follows the English tradition whereby the Lord Chief Justice assumed responsibility for most of the big criminal appeals and the Master of the Rolls most major civil appeals',[95] there is also a Northern Ireland-specific reason for the Chief Justice's 'particularly strong'[96] role in sentencing appeals. The reason is that in the absence of schematic Crown Court sentencing guidelines in Northern Ireland, if there is a point to be decided about 'the policy of the courts on drugs', for example, it is thought to

---

[89] J5. For our analysis of dissenting judgments in the Court of Appeal, see Chapter 3.

[90] J7.

[91] J2; J4; J7.

[92] J2.

[93] J7.

[94] J5.

[95] J5. The judge acknowledged that, of course, there is no Master of the Rolls in Northern Ireland.

[96] J7.

be particularly important that that policy 'should come from the Chief Justice'.[97]

Interestingly, though perhaps unsurprisingly, we found that the judges we spoke to recognised different leadership styles among those who have held office as President of the Court of Appeal. For instance, whereas one President was described as 'quite a consensus-driven individual',[98] another was characterised as a 'results-driven' and 'policy-minded' office-holder.[99] We hope to explore these observations in greater depth at some point in the future, together with further research on the many more non-contentious matters for which the Court's President is responsible, but let it suffice to note here that we have come to regard the role as a seriously 'tough ticket'[100] simply by virtue of the multifarious volume of work involved.

8.5 Conclusion

This chapter has canvassed the extent to which our judicial interviewees would either conserve or reform various aspects of the way the Court of Appeal operates.

In the statutory realm, it has charted how some judges are keener than others on wholesale reform of the Court's governing legislation. At a more itemised level, it has revealed that there is a strong degree of consensus around proposals to replace the rules in respect of judicial review appeals involving criminal causes or matters. There is less outright support for proposals to require leave to appeal in all civil cases and to expand the scope of appeal rights for cases that begin in inferior courts and tribunals, though, as with all the

---

[97] J7; also see Chapter 5.
[98] J2.
[99] J3.
[100] As J4 put it.

statutory proposals, there are interesting reasons and nuanced reservations underlying these generalised conclusions. Views are quite clearly mixed when it comes to the size of the Court of Appeal, both as limited in individual cases and as limited overall. Some judges see no problem with two-person panels, whereas others would prefer to see three-person panels used in practically every case. Likewise, there are judges who think there is now a business case that would justify appointing a fourth Lord or Lady Justice of Appeal, while some are more doubtful about whether such a step is necessary.

In the non-statutory realm, there is also a high degree of consensus around proposals to conserve and strengthen a strict approach to practitioners' non-compliance with Practice Directions and case management direction orders. There seems to be agreement around the President's powers to choose appeal panel members and to take the lead in writing certain categories of case, though there was a lesser degree of consensus as regards the President's policy of assigning lead judgment writers very early in the administration of each case.

In both the statutory and non-statutory sections of the chapter, certain proposals were noted notwithstanding that only one or two judges discussed them with us and that they were recognised as relatively low priorities. This category included proposals to empower the Court to sit as a panel of five in appropriate cases, proposals to empower the Court to refer parties for arbitration or mediation, and proposals to enable the broadcasting of sentencing remarks.

As the last-mentioned category of proposals highlights so clearly, all of the judges we spoke to exhibited a propensity to balance idealism with pragmatism. This propensity was evident in the judges' efforts to identify reform proposals according to different levels of priority. It was likewise evident in the 'make do and mend' approach that was adopted by several interviewees in respect of the Court's governing legislation. We are sure that this same propensity will make it possible for the Court to settle whatever disagreements may exist or arise among its members by way of further conversation and debate. We hope that mapping the independently formed opinions of its judges, as we have attempted here, will usefully inform and advance those discussions.

NINE

Conclusion

Around the world there are hundreds of appeal courts charged with a responsibility for upholding the standards of justice expected from lower courts and tribunals, but there are relatively few scholarly studies on how those courts operate.[1] Understandably, the scholarship is particularly sparse as regards appeal courts in smaller jurisdictions. This volume on the Court of Appeal in Northern Ireland has sought to convey a contextualised sense of how one intermediate appellate court goes about its business and to investigate its effectiveness by reference to several standpoints. Having explained in Chapter 2 the historical context in which the Court of Appeal was established over 100 years ago, together with an outline of significant turning points relevant to its development, subsequent chapters have interrogated the role of the Court over the past 25 years – the post Belfast (Good Friday) Agreement period.

This focus on the Court's recent history has generated interesting findings regarding specific issues that have confronted the Court by virtue of its unique duty to serve a society emerging from violent conflict and periodically afflicted

---

[1] For an exceptionally useful overview of appellate processes in the US, South Africa, Australia, New Zealand, Canada, France, Italy, the Netherlands, Norway, and Israel, see Louis Blom-Cooper and Gavin Drewry, *Final Appeal: A Study of the House of Lords in its Judicial Capacity* (Clarendon Press 1972) 51–60. See also Brice Dickson (ed), *Judicial Activism in Common Law Supreme Courts* (Oxford University Press 2007).

by political instability. Following a macro-level analysis of the Court's caseload in Chapter 3, Chapter 4 explained its civil business (including an extensive judicial review portfolio). Chapter 5 then considered its criminal business (including a jurisprudentially challenging jurisdiction for deciding whether historic convictions should in certain circumstances be overturned by reference to modern-day standards). The sheer variety of legal disputes that the Court of Appeal has been required to contend with over the past quarter of a century – and the care it has taken to apply and develop standards for considering them with appropriately calibrated levels of invasiveness – is evident from these analyses.

Chapter 6 reinforced this assessment by spotlighting particularly conspicuous cases that have passed through the Court since the Belfast (Good Friday) Agreement and by referring to reputable commentators who have praised or criticised the Court for its decisions on different occasions. Chapter 7 continued with this theme by evaluating the Court's efficacy from the perspective of the highest court in the land; that is, the Appellate Committee of the House of Lords and (since 2009) the Supreme Court which succeeded it. It showed that while the Court of Appeal has been overturned many times, statistically it has fared no worse than its analogue in England and Wales. Finally, Chapter 8 enumerated various judicial preferences about the legislative framework for the Court, its non-statutory practices and procedures, and the role of its President.

At this point, rather than rehearsing the detailed findings from each of those chapters, we think it is fitting to conclude by highlighting three potentially under-appreciated themes that run throughout them. The first is an appreciation for the finality of the Court of Appeal's decisions in many contexts given that in certain circumstances no further appeals are permitted, as with most cases stated from the county court,[2]

---

[2]   County Courts (NI) Order 1980, art 61(7).

and in others there is only a slim chance of a further appeal by virtue of the restrictive test that is applied to cases intended for the Supreme Court; namely, does the case 'raise an arguable point of law of general public importance'.[3] On this account, we see some educational merit in a theory of the entire appellate court system which, as Blom-Cooper and Drewry once suggested, understands it 'not so much in terms of a hierarchy of increasing judicial authority, but as a series of concentric spheres of influence'.[4]

Relatedly, we consider it worth emphasising that when deciding the many cases which reach their conclusion before it, the Court of Appeal typically discharges one of two roles. The first is a reviewing role, which involves 'correcting mistakes at first instance' and 'creating some kind of continuity, consistency, and certainty in the administration of justice'.[5] The second is a supervisory role, which entails 'laying down fresh precedents and updating old ones for the guidance of lower courts'.[6] Based on our reading of its judgments, it seems clear that the Court of Appeal in Northern Ireland has been performing each of those functions fairly effectively.

The third and final theme running through this book is an appreciation for the variety and complexity of the work that is carried out by the Court of Appeal in Northern Ireland. It is a highly professionalised and self-aware judicial body, and,

---

[3] UK Supreme Court, Practice Direction 3, para 3.3.3.

[4] Blom-Cooper and Drewry, n 1, 64. See also Gavin Drewry, Louis Blom-Cooper, and Charles Blake, *The Court of Appeal* (Hart Publishing 2007) 185, where the authors conclude that '[i]t would be only a slight exaggeration to say that, whatever the formal organisation chart of the courts hierarchy [in England and Wales] may suggest, there are now, in effect, two "final" courts of appeal'.

[5] Charles Blake and Gavin Drewry, 'The Role of the Court of Appeal in England and Wales as an Intermediate Court' in Andrew Le Sueur (ed), *Building the UK's New Supreme Court: National and Comparative Perspectives* (Oxford University Press 2004) 226.

[6] Ibid.

given the level of complexity that inheres in the substantive law and legal procedures for this jurisdiction, it needs to be. Whereas the Supreme Court has been characterised as 'a court of specialists',[7] meaning a court which consists of legal subject area specialists,[8] the Court of Appeal in Northern Ireland should in our opinion be viewed as 'a court of generalists', given that its permanent members are effectively required to be masters or mistresses of all trades.

All in all, while it shares common features with its counterparts elsewhere in the UK and beyond, we have come to regard the Court of Appeal in Northern Ireland as a singular institution operating 'a distinct jurisdiction' for 'a different place'.[9]

[7] Chris Hanretty, *A Court of Specialists: Judicial Behaviour on the UK Supreme Court* (Oxford University Press 2020).

[8] Ibid, passim.

[9] J7.

APPENDIX A

Who Succeeded Whom as Lord/Lady Chief Justice of Northern Ireland (and President of the Court of Appeal)

Sir Denis Henry 1921–25
Sir William Moore 1925–37*
Sir James Andrews 1937–51*
Lord MacDermott 1951–71
Sir Robert Lowry 1971–88
Sir Brian Hutton 1988–97
Sir Robert Carswell 1997–2004*
Sir Brian Kerr 2004–09
Sir Declan Morgan 2009–21
Dame Siobhan Keegan 2021–

* Indicates that the person was formerly a Lord Justice of Appeal.
Lord MacDermott was formerly a Lord of Appeal in Ordinary.

APPENDIX B

Who Succeeded Whom as a Lord Justice of Appeal in Northern Ireland

1	2	3
Sir William Moore 1921–25*	Sir James Andrews 1921–37*	Sir Ambrose McGonigal 1975–79
Richard Best 1925–39	Sir Anthony Babington 1937–49	Turlough O'Donnell 1979–89
Edward Murphy 1939–45	Arthur Black 1949–64	Sir Donald Murray 1989–93
Samuel Porter 1946–56	Sir Herbert McVeigh 1964–73	Sir Eoin Higgins 1993
Sir Lancelot Curran 1956–75	Sir Edward Jones 1973–84	Sir Robert Carswell 1993–97*
Sir Maurice Gibson 1975–87	Sir Basil Kelly 1984–95	Sir Liam McCollum 1997–2004
Sir John MacDermott 1987–98	Sir Michael Nicholson 1995–2007	Sir John Sheil 2004–07
Sir Anthony Campbell 1998–2008	Sir Malachy Higgins 2007–14	Sir Paul Girvan 2007–15
Sir Patrick Coghlin 2008–15	Sir John Gillen 2014–17	Sir Ronald Weatherup 2015–17
Sir Reginald Weir 2015–17	Sir Seamus Treacy 2017–	Sir Donnell Deeny 2017–19

1	2	3
Sir Benjamin Stephens 2017–20		Sir Bernard McCloskey 2019–
Sir Paul Maguire 2021–22		
Sir Mark Horner 2022–		

* Indicates that the person later became the Lord Chief Justice.
Sir Robert Carswell also went on to become a Lord of Appeal in Ordinary
and Sir Benjamin Stephens went on to become a Justice of the UK Supreme
Court. Sir John MacDermott was the son of Lord MacDermott, a former Lord
Chief Justice. A son of Turlough O'Donnell is the current Chief Justice of Ireland.

APPENDIX C

The Changing Composition of the Court of Appeal in Northern Ireland

1921	Henry LCJ, Moore LJ, Andrews LJ
1925	Moore LCJ, Andrews LJ, Best LJ
1937	Andrews LCJ, Best LJ, Babington LJ
1939	Andrews LCJ, Babington LJ, Murphy LJ
1946	Andrews LCJ, Babington LJ, Porter LJ
1949	Andrews LCJ, Porter LJ, Black LJ
1951	MacDermott LCJ, Porter LJ, Black LJ
1956	MacDermott LCJ, Black LJ, Curran LJ
1964	MacDermott LCJ, Curran LJ, McVeigh LJ
1971	Lowry LCJ, Curran LJ, McVeigh LJ
1973	Lowry LCJ, Curran LJ, Jones LJ
1975	Lowry LCJ, Jones LJ, Gibson LJ, McGonigal LJ
1979	Lowry LCJ, Jones LJ, Gibson LJ, O'Donnell LJ
1984	Lowry LCJ, Gibson LJ, O'Donnell LJ, Kelly LJ
1987	Lowry LCJ, O'Donnell LJ, Kelly LJ, MacDermott LJ
1988	Hutton LCJ, O'Donnell LJ, Kelly LJ, MacDermott LJ
1989	Hutton LCJ, Kelly LJ, MacDermott LJ, Murray LJ
1993	Hutton LCJ, Kelly LJ, MacDermott LJ, Carswell LJ
1995	Hutton LCJ, MacDermott LJ, Carswell LJ, Nicholson LJ

1997	Carswell LCJ, MacDermott LJ, Nicholson LJ, McCollum LJ
1998	Carswell LCJ, Nicholson LJ, McCollum LJ, Campbell LJ
2004	Kerr LCJ, Nicholson LJ, Campbell LJ, Sheil LJ
2007	Kerr LCJ, Campbell LJ, Higgins LJ, Girvan LJ
2008	Kerr LCJ, Higgins LJ, Girvan LJ, Coghlin LJ
2009	Morgan LCJ, Higgins LJ, Girvan LJ, Coghlin LJ
2014	Morgan LCJ, Girvan LJ, Coghlin LJ, Gillen LJ
2015	Morgan LCJ, Gillen LJ, Weatherup LJ, Weir LJ
2017	Morgan LCJ, Stephens LJ, Deeny LJ, Treacy LJ
2019	Morgan LCJ, Stephens LJ, Treacy LJ, McCloskey LJ
2021	Keegan LCJ, Treacy LJ, McCloskey LJ, Maguire LJ
2022	Keegan LCJ, Treacy LJ, McCloskey LJ, Horner LJ

This list does not treat separately appointments made at different times within the same year. Each line denotes the composition of the Court at the end of the year shown.

Index

References to tables appear in **bold** type. References to footnotes show both the page number and the note number (132n28).